# Begin Your Psychic Journey

# Begin Your Psychic Journey

◆

## Discovering the Path to Your Intuitive Gifts

*Rebecca Bloom*

iUniverse, Inc.
New York  Lincoln  Shanghai

# Begin Your Psychic Journey
## Discovering the Path to Your Intuitive Gifts

iUniverse, Inc.

For information address:
iUniverse, Inc.
2021 Pine Lake Road, Suite 100
Lincoln, NE 68512
www.iuniverse.com

ISBN: 0-595-29283-6

Printed in the United States of America

Dedicated to Clarissa and Rosie, without whom I would not have fully uncovered my own intuitive gifts, and to all of my students: past, present, and future.

# *Contents*

Learn how to begin the inner journeying process. Discover the importance of deepening the connection with your physical body as you start to open up your psychic side, as well as ways to cleanse and condition yourself so that you recognize intuitive messages.

Practice a rejuvenating loop breathing technique, correct common problems that often occur, and find out how to stay grounded while meditating. Two scripted meditations full of wonderful guided imagery help you master your own meditative style.

In order to progress along your psychic path and implicitly trust your soul's voice, you need to acknowledge where you are in your current stage of spiritual development. A descriptive writing exercise gives you important feedback for future use.

Now you are ready to experiment further with your energy, specifically the energy you project into the outside world. Learn four powerful techniques to help you practice seeing auras and try a method for tangibly feeling them too.

Focusing on your complex and mysterious chakras is next. All seven of them reveal an immense amount of information about your psychic state of being. Discover useful ways to keep them healthy and vibrant.

Now that you have a well-rounded knowledge base of your psychic abilities
and how you can use them in your day-to-day activities, you may wish to
explore other metaphysical tools. Read descriptions of these additional
methods to help you decide your next step.

# *Introduction*

Welcome! This book was developed in response to my students' many requests for a down-to-earth, thorough guide to help them uncover and strengthen their intuitive processes and psychic abilities. The format of this book follows that of my thirteen-week Psychic Development Class and is designed to gently escort you through a series of increasingly more advanced metaphysical exercises and techniques. By doing each chapter in order, you will build a well-rounded, solid foundation of metaphysical theory and your psychic abilities will begin to expand and blossom. I named my company *Blooming Insights* to reflect my philosophy that everyone is psychic—your intention to reveal your spiritual gifts gives birth to the process that integrates your intuitive side with your day-to-day activities. I truly believe that this type of integration creates a more satisfying way to walk down our life path.

Have fun with this book and do not become discouraged if at first some of the exercises or techniques seem difficult. In developing our psychic side, it is common for certain modalities to come easily and others to initially seem out of reach. The hard-to-reach techniques will fall into place with practice; for example, I did not master reading auras until a year or two into my initial training. Never give up and be sure to allow yourself the freedom to learn and expand *at your own pace*. By honoring your individual timetable, you honor your personal psychic process.

I wish you much success on your inner journey—in fact, view this book as an "inner" vacation! Experimenting with the exercises in this guide does involve effort and persistence, but you will experience similar rejuvenating benefits as those gained from a relaxing trip. My primary goal is to help you challenge your intuitive and psychic selves in a way that feels relaxing, growth-oriented, and enjoyable.

Rebecca Bloom

# 1

# *Preparing for Inner Change*

Congratulations to you for deciding to pursue your spiritual growth through psychic development! To do so is a very exciting and educational process. Before we start, it is important to first take care of some basic ideas and suggestions that will help you prepare yourself for uncovering and strengthening your intuitive side.

## Take Care of Your Constitutional Health

Because you are in the process of expanding your intuitive awareness and psychic abilities, it is important to take extra care of your physical self. Performing regular meditative sessions and practicing the other exercises contained in this book use more energy than you are probably accustomed to expending. Good constitutional health supports the inner work you will be doing and allows you to more easily understand and master the techniques. As an adjunct to your psychic studies, be sure to eat a nutritionally sound diet, get enough sleep, exercise regularly, and take vitamin or herbal supplements as required. And by all means, never push yourself to practice meditating or execute a particular exercise if you feel physically ill. The body is a temple and we need to honor its need to heal and rejuvenate when we are fighting a virus, dealing with a muscle strain, or recuperating from anything else that tends to sideline us for a short time. You may also find it helpful to eat a light snack before practicing an intuitive technique—or right after if you plan on going on to another exercise without a break.

## Emotional Connections to Physiological Illnesses

Even when we take care of our constitutional health, illnesses and injuries still occur. Because human beings are sensitive and impressionable creatures, most of us care deeply about other people and are affected by the actions of those around us. Since the integration of mind, body, and spirit is so key to becoming fully satisfied with all aspects of our lives, it makes sense that the physical body becomes temporarily impaired when something causes us to be emotionally off balance. The more easily we can pinpoint the emotional connection to a physiological illness, the shorter the duration of that illness and the less likely that illness will crop up again for the same reason. For example, if you are prone to sore throats, try reflecting on how your throat area is used (i.e., for communication). Is there something you need to say? How about stomachaches? What are you currently doing that you cannot "stomach?"

Take a moment right now to remember the last three times your physical body got hurt or you fought a cold or flu bug. It may help to jot these down. Be sure to list all details and symptoms, no matter how minor they may seem. Can you draw a parallel between what occurred physiologically and what you experienced emotionally? Seeing your conclusions in black and white may further jar your memory and allow you to remember significant, emotional turning points or upheavals that coincided with an actual illness or injury. In fact, many people experience "light bulb" moments when doing this exercise and can more definitively identify correlations whose origins can be traced back to infancy.

The association between illness and emotions also relates to the right and left sides of the body (see discussion later in this chapter). For example, if you hurt your right arm or leg, think about your fears as they relate to going out into the world to take care of business or to display your talents. If you tend to get headaches that cluster on the left side, it could be a signal that you may be doing too much internal self-reflection; it might help to discuss your concerns or ideas with another person and not hold everything in. By understanding that most physi-ological illnesses have emotional components at their roots, we can heal ourselves more quickly and with greater insight for future occurrences.

*[Note: student names and exact ages in this book have been changed to pro-tect their privacy.]*

*Linda, 25, was a medical receptionist in a busy, multi-physician office. A very personable young woman, she interacted with all types of people on a daily basis. Linda enjoyed greeting patients as they came through the door and often took the time to exchange pleasantries with them. Her personal life, however, caused her quite a bit of distress. She had been dating a man for the past year and was beginning to feel more and more uncomfortable with their relationship. Linda found herself getting caught up in numerous arguments with her boyfriend over the same issues. They just couldn't see eye to eye and resolve their differences.*

*One morning, Linda woke up to find a slight skin discoloration under her left eye. Thinking that perhaps a bug had bitten her during the night, she simply put on a bit more makeup and went off to work. But at night as she washed up, Linda saw that the discoloration had progressed into a bright red, eczema-like patch of skin. Alarmed, she found the phone num-ber for a dermatologist in her health plan and put it on her dresser so she could make an appointment in the morning.*

*The dermatologist diagnosed the red swatch as contact dermatitis and prescribed a cortisone cream. Over the next few weeks however, Linda's skin condition got worse instead of better. The rash was now tender to the touch, oozed fluid at times, and felt hot. Linda's doctor was perplexed and had her try other topical agents, all to no avail. Becoming increasingly frus-trated, Linda also sought treatment from an herbalist who applied herbal compresses to the irritation under her left eye. Nothing seemed to help. Her condition began to affect her work performance since Linda felt extremely self-conscious as she interacted with the patients. Applying extra makeup over the dermatitis was no longer working. Almost three months went by and Linda was soon at her wits' end.*

*I helped Linda draw a parallel between her severe rash and her unsatis-factory relationship with her boyfriend. Telling her that our skin is the last physical chance for us to see that something is amiss in our lives, any form of skin condition—like acne or eczema—can often be a visual "cry for help." I asked Linda if she ever cried in frustration, either alone or during argu-ments with her partner. She responded that it was hard for her to release in this manner. I suggested that allowing herself to weep might release pent-up feelings that she could then express to her boyfriend. Linda remembered a class lecture where I described how the left side of our bodies deals with emotions. This helped her to understand why the angry-looking, red patch of skin appeared under her left eye. Her emotional suppression needed to end!*

*Little by little, Linda gained the courage to express herself more honestly and she and her boyfriend began to communicate more effectively with one another. Once Linda made the commitment to release her feelings through words and crying, her patch of severe dermatitis completely cleared up within one week. Linda's bout with a very trying and long-lasting skin condition taught her how physical illnesses usually have an emotional com-ponent. When she took the time to find the connection, she was able to heal herself that much faster.*

## Right vs. Left Sides of the Body

In many of the intuition-enhancing exercises in this book, noting what is happening on both sides of your body (or that of your subject's, if you are working with a partner) is important. There is a metaphysical theory that states all human beings are comprised of both male and female energy. This gender-specific energy is represented by either the left or right side of the body. Our left side houses our female qualities, which encompass receptivity, intuition, emotions, and introspection. The right side incorporates our male qualities, which include giving, logic, taking care of business, and working with the external environ-ment. For example, if you see an aura that is stronger on the right side of the body, you are wanting and needing to address issues of intellect and interaction with the outside world. Conversely, if your aura is stronger on your left side, you are working through issues that involve your emotions, psychicness, and being open to receiving messages from your inner voice.

Including the interpretation of right vs. left sides of the body in psychic techniques will help you immensely in figuring out more about yourself. Try to remember to check both sides of your body when performing the exercises in this book and you will find yourself growing and expanding at an accelerated pace. The more symbolic information we gather, the easier it becomes to interpret psychic messages.

## Journal into Your Heart and Soul

Since this book introduces you to such a wide variety of growth-oriented exercises, it is also an excellent time to start a combination dream journal and diary. This journal-diary works best if you designate a special notebook for this purpose and only enter into it your dreams, thoughts, experiences, and results from practicing the techniques. It is very important to record what bubbles up from your soul and subconscious. Do not include shopping lists or notes from a class! In addition, be sure to always date your entries. During the psychic-expanding process you will likely receive many messages from your higher self and it is important to track these messages and images in your notebook. You will begin to see repeated patterns and you can then more easily interpret them. These patterns are extremely helpful for working through old, emotional blocks and for understanding what you need to move toward a fulfilling spiritual life.

## Honoring Your Hermit Side

Do not be surprised if you find yourself needing more private time as you delve deeper into your psychic self. This is normal. You are breaking through very old thought patterns and attitudes about yourself, your life, and the world. You need the increased solo time to purge that which is no longer you. Giving yourself permission to schedule more time for yourself allows you to free up and hear more intuitive messages. In the Tarot cards, The Hermit is always depicted as a wise person holding some sort of light source, like a lantern or torch. This light source symbolizes the conduit for going within to uncover more answers about our inner development. So, do not hesitate to cancel social engagements and ask your loved ones to honor your requests for more time to yourself.

## Sea Salt Washes

One inexpensive item to purchase that will assist your core energy as it begins to expand and solidify is sea salt. Different from iodized table salt, sea salt allows you to instantly cleanse and become grounded (refer to Chapter 2). You can buy sea salt in bulk at most health food stores. The small-grained variety, which looks like table salt, is best.

Place a small dish of sea salt by each of the sinks in your home. To cleanse the day's energy out of your system (including interactions with both positive and difficult people), simply take a couple of pinches and place in the palms of your hands before wetting them. Rub the salt gently between your palms and then rinse your hands. This easy technique is extremely effective for fully reclaiming your energy and it prepares you for practicing meditation and other exercises. You can also use sea salt in the shower. If you have had a particularly trying day, stand in the shower and rub a bit of the salt all over your body—including your scalp—and then rinse. Sea salt is a true gift that helps us transition from the day and cleanse away the energy we are bombarded with on a daily basis.

## Receiving Psychic Information

Did you know we possess five psychic senses that correspond to our five physical senses? Because psychic/intuitive information can come to us in a variety of ways, it helps to be aware of how we can receive these messages. Our five physical senses are comprised of sight, touch, taste, hear, and smell. Our five psychic senses operate on all of these levels too; for instance, some of us hear our messages, some smell certain odors that evoke a deep symbolic meaning, and others feel an answer to a question by touching an object or a person's hand. By staying open to how you may receive psychic information, you will be less likely to miss or second-guess what you are seeing, feeling, hearing, tasting, or smelling.

It is also interesting to note that whichever of your senses seems most strong at present may change as you continue to evolve. This is where your notebook can play an important role: jot down any and all psychic snippets you receive at any given time and keep track of how you received the information. By snippets, I am referring to fleeting pieces of information that seem disconnected or do not seem like an entire message. Examples of snippets can be seeing a wash of color or hearing one word or a short phrase. Very rarely does psychic information come to us as a full sentence or as a complete scene played out in our mind's eye. Interpreting our psychic messages comes down, in large part, to recognizing how we usually receive our information and then in knowing what particular symbols mean *to us*. Can you remember any recent psychic impressions? Through which sense, or senses, did they occur? At your leisure, reflect upon your experiences to date—in the near future it will be interesting to note how your receptivity changes and deepens.

Be sensitive to your five psychic senses as you proceed through this book. Give yourself the freedom to experience in your own way and at your own pace. Psychic development is very individualized and personal and you will experience many "light bulb" moments and increased joy as you progress on your journey.

Becoming more psychically aware is similar to being a detective. Instead of gathering facts about time, place, and modus operandi, you will be uncovering details about your inner workings (and possibly the inner workings of others). Consider how paying attention to the above topics can support this process.

# 2

## *Meditation: Harnessing Energy & Receiving Messages*

Learning to meditate lays the foundation for both tapping directly into your psychic side, which contains important growth-oriented messages, and preparing yourself for metaphysical techniques and exercises. And, contrary to some misconceptions, meditation does not need to be approached like a daily chore; actually, if done correctly, you will find yourself feeling somewhat incomplete and out of sorts when you miss a session. Your body and soul will begin to crave the nurturing act of letting yourself truly relax and rejuvenate.

### Benefits of Meditation

- Replenishes energy—no matter what time of day or night.
- Clears the mind—gives us a break from noise pollution and demands of home and office.
- Lowers blood pressure.
- Slows the aging process.
- Creates a quiet space to receive messages from our higher selves.
- Prepares us for doing other psychic techniques.
- Best of all—it's free!

## Basic Meditation

So, how often and how long does one need to meditate? I follow the metaphysical school of thought that short meditations can be just as beneficial as those of longer length—the key is to practice regularly, at least five times per week. To produce the most results, allow approximately fifteen minutes for each session. If at first you feel resistant to the meditative process, you most likely are experiencing one or more challenges commonly associated with learning how to meditate. Review the points below to see if you recognize any of the obstacles listed.

### Common Challenges Beginners Face

- Mind wandering: gently tell yourself you will think about the particular topic later.

- Trouble finding a comfortable position: try sitting on a rug with a pillow supporting your buttocks and lower back, lying on your back, or sitting on a comfortable chair.

- Being physically uncomfortable: wear loose clothing, take shoes off, even try meditating in the nude!

- Uncomfortable environment: light candles, burn incense, and play relaxing, ethereal, background music to create an inviting setting.

- Not scheduling a regular, special time: experiment with different times to find the most convenient and then stick with this sacred period that is for you alone.

- Not breathing deeply enough or not grounding: practice a little more and these will soon become second nature. (Instruction to follow.)

- Trying too hard: allow yourself the patience and time to develop this new skill. Remind yourself of the benefits and that you are giving yourself a gift of private time.

- Trying when physically sick: even though meditating can help ease the discomfort of constitutional illness, if you are feeling too uncomfortable, take a break and return to regular sessions after the illness has passed from your body.

- Not being in a relaxed state: try repeating this affirmation, "I am calm and relaxed and am open to receive any and all information."

## Take a Deep, Cleansing Breath

Breathing properly during meditation is key to releasing more of your intuitive and psychic abilities. Most of us breathe very shallowly, working only the lungs and upper chest cavity. But for meditation and accessing information from deep within our psychic core, we must utilize the whole torso. I call this type of breathing "loop" breathing, because we start the air at our abdomen, continue the breath upward to expand our chest, up to our head, and then back down the spine, finishing again at our abdomen. This technique is actually the same process used by highly trained vocalists. Here are the steps:

### Loop Breathing Technique

- Sit or stand comfortably in loose clothing.

- Place one hand on your abdomen and one on your chest.

- Close your eyes and take a few, deep breaths.

- On the next inhalation, begin by distending your stomach—not your chest—with the air. Check the hand over your abdomen to make sure it is moving outward. [Note: women can pretend they are pregnant, men can pretend they have just eaten a large meal.]

- Draw the air from the same inhalation upward, filling the lower rib cage, then the chest. Feel the hand on your chest move outward.

- Continue drawing the air up to the top of your head and pause slightly.

- Begin to exhale and start to bring the breath down the back of your head, down your spine as it passes in back of your chest (the hand over your chest now pushes inward), behind your rib-cage and, finally, behind your abdomen (the hand over your abdomen pushes the remaining air out by pressing in).

- Relax, then begin the loop again with the next inhalation.

[Note: it helps at first to make exaggerated breath sounds as you do the loop. This allows you to more easily track your breath.]

Go as slowly as you can to gain the most benefit. At first, you may feel dizzy or lightheaded; this is because you are getting more air into your system than you do with shallow, chest-only breathing. Practice once or twice a day for approximately ten minutes each session. Many people find first thing in the morning or right before retiring a good time to dedicate to this exercise. As with learning anything new, regular practice makes the technique easier, and it will soon become second nature. This type of deep breathing not only prepares you for meditation and other focusing techniques, but also enhances your physical body by fully oxygenating your cells. Mastering loop breathing will allow you to clear your mind, rejuvenate your body, and tell your psychic self you are ready to receive input.

## Grounding

Besides practicing and mastering loop breathing, it is also very important to ground yourself before each meditation and before performing most intuition-enhancing exercises. Grounding is necessary because we do not want to get too heady while meditating; instead we want to have an anchor that allows us to focus and be fully receptive to our inner voice. By grounding, we tell our subconscious we are safely connected to our environment. Only then can we truly let go and let our mind and soul expand.

One of the easiest and most helpful grounding images consists of utilizing the natural world. After you start your loop breathing, in your mind's eye send out tree roots from the base of your spine and the soles of your feet. These tree roots continue to flow out of you and then go through the floor, your home's foundation and, finally, anchor deep within Mother Earth.

Another grounding image that can be used solely or in connection with the tree roots imagery consists of imagining a star floating down from the heavens and pausing about three feet above your head. This star then begins to send out white rays of light that fall all around you and secure themselves into Mother Earth. You are gently surrounded by these white rays and they serve as grounding energy.

Experiment with both of these grounding techniques to see which feels most comfortable. The important point is to ground before beginning a meditation; by doing this, you will experience greater satisfaction with the process and your meditative sessions will be much more productive.

To help you get started, reproduced below is a script from one of my popular guided meditations. When learning how to meditate, staying focused is a typical challenge for many people. The Candle Meditation allows you to practice your focusing skills. It may be helpful for you to record this script onto an audiocassette and play it for yourself during meditative sessions. It will also be beneficial to jot down your experiences after initially performing this meditation; in your journal, describe what you saw during the narrative and, afterward, how you felt. Did you gain a greater sense of peace? Were you able to quiet distracting thoughts while gazing at the candle? This will become easier over time.

**Candle Meditation—Read Very Slowly—Time: 8–10 Minutes**
***Before you begin this meditation, you will need to light a candle and set it on a table in front of you.***

And now we begin…sit or recline comfortably…close your eyes…and ground yourself by sending out tree roots from the soles of your feet and the base of your spine…have these tree roots go through the floor and anchor them deeply into Mother Earth…slow your breath down and take very deep breaths, filling your lungs and torso completely…**[pause for 1.5 minutes]**…continue to relax…and gently release any thoughts about what happened earlier in the day or yesterday…gently release any thoughts about what you need to do later or tomorrow…release tension from any part of your body by sending your breath there…**[pause for 30 seconds]**…continue to relax, slowing the breath down…focus on feeling how your breath circulates throughout your body…**[pause for 1 minute]**…now slowly open your eyes until you're looking directly at the candle on the table in front of you…simply gaze at the candle flame…feel yourself very relaxed as you're gazing at the candle flame…note how the flame looks: its colors, how it moves and vibrates slightly, the brightness of it…continue gazing peacefully at the candle flame…now notice its wick and where the wick joins to the top of the candle…continue to gaze at the candle flame…**[pause for 1 minute]**…does the flame seem bigger now?…does the flame seem brighter?…now slowly close your eyelids and see the candle flame on the back of your eyelids…note how it looks this way…do you see the outline of the candle?…are there any other colors produced with your eyes closed?…is there any movement in the image?…continue to relax with your eyelids closed…**[pause for 1 minute]**…now slowly reopen your eyelids and gaze peacefully again at the candle flame…note its colors again and its movement…now slowly close your eyelids one more time and take a super deep, cleansing breath…and take another super deep, cleansing breath…and take another super deep, cleansing breath and stretch your arms up and over your head…and you can open your eyes when you feel ready.

Take your time during subsequent Candle Meditation practice sessions and remember to stay open to any messages, symbols, or images you receive. As stated earlier, psychic information may come in a variety of ways through your five psychic senses. You may see a picture or scene in your mind's eye, smell a particular scent, or hear sounds or words, just to name a few common occurrences.

## Start a Color Log

As you may have noticed, during meditation it is common to see colors in certain shapes, such as sparks or elongated blobs. This is energy moving both from and around your body. In your journal, keep track of what colors and shapes you receive. To enhance your understanding of how color plays a key role in deciphering psychic information, start an official Color Log. This log consists of a running list of various colors and their personal meanings to you. For instance, if you think of the color yellow, how does this make you feel? Upbeat? Sunny? Optimistic? Calm? Your Color Log contains your point-blank emotional responses to various hues. Knowing your personal color symbolism will help with future interpretations of intuitive information. Colors often come into play when performing psychic exercises, like reading auras. Jot down three or four colors each day and have fun with this project. You can get as creative as you like; for example, include more unusual shades like teal, chartreuse, and peach. Here is a sample of a Color Log:

### Color Log

Blue—calming, communication, wisdom

Red—strength, passion, anger, grounding

Purple—psychic, royalty, soothing

Brown—earthy, muddy, natural

Yellow—fresh start, fear, optimistic

White—pure, ethereal, higher power

Green—growth, prosperity, integration

Orange—creative, fresh, energetic

## Meditating in Nature

Did you know that meditating outdoors can produce a very different experience than practicing indoors? Placing ourselves in the midst of a natural environment can help us more freely access our psychic core. Try leaning against a tree, perching on top of a boulder, or sitting on the sand at the shore of a peaceful stretch of coastline. Even meditating in your backyard will produce beneficial and rejuvenating results. Remember, of course, to ground first and then begin your loop breathing. Record in your journal your experiences, paying particular attention to any images, thoughts, and symbols. Also, jot down your location and time of day. Since meditating in nature often produces crystal-clear messages from your inner voice, you may, at a later date, want to do a second practice session under the exact same conditions.

*Chleo, 53, was an attorney with an impressive track record. During her career, she won many civil rights cases and, early on, had gained the respect and admiration of her colleagues and key, liberal, national leaders. She felt very driven to succeed and fight for her clients. What did Chleo do to rejuvenate and replenish her energy? Hardly anything. This woman with the Type A+ personality had an extremely difficult time allowing herself to relax.*

*I knew my homework assignment of asking the class to write about their experiences during a nature meditation would be difficult for Chleo. Not only was I asking her to be still and go within, I was also asking her to take the time to drive somewhere, away from her comfortable home and urban environment. But she graciously accepted the challenge and actually sur-*

*prised me with the depth and beauty of her descriptions and ability to put words to her inner voice. The following is taken verbatim from her journal:*

*"I decided to drive up to the mountains and try to find a particular meadow I remembered visiting as a teenager. Not quite sure which turnoff to take, I let my memory and intuition guide me. I was so happy when I recognized the narrow dirt road! I parked my car and walked the short way to the entrance of the meadow. As soon as I saw the familiar scene, with the large oak tree off to the right and a small stream flowing a few yards from its base, I knew I had found my meditation spot. The rest of the meadow looked and felt great—the grass was lush and fragrant, there was a slight warm breeze blowing through the other trees and bushes, and I could even hear a few birds calling to one another.*

*"I sat with my back against the oak tree and took off my shoes. I closed my eyes and began to take deep breaths, which soon turned into the loop breathing technique. When I sent out tree roots to ground myself, I was surprised at how they looked in my mind's eye. During class, my tree roots are of medium width and are a medium brown color. But this time they were thicker, more knobby, and were a rich golden brown. I could really feel them coming out of my spine and bottoms of my feet, going deep through the grass and into the earth. And leaning against the oak tree helped to ground me even further. I felt warmth coming from its bark and my back felt cradled. With my eyes closed, I could feel the life force within the tree and it felt very nurturing.*

*"I decided that with this nature meditation, I would let myself become still and allow whatever messages that needed to come in to do so. As I became more relaxed, the sound of the stream running nearby became more pronounced, and I could even hear the difference in the water's tone as it passed over various sizes of rocks and pebbles. And the chirping of the birds sounded more conversation-like with my eyes closed. I imagined them planning their afternoon activities.*

*"Pretty soon, I began to receive messages from my inner voice. I distinctly heard the phrase, 'You need to honor your quiet times'. My higher self also said, 'Taking a break will help you with your work.' I was surprised to*

*hear this second message, since I was in the middle of a very trying, time-consuming case. I relaxed for a little while longer and I could feel my blood pressure lowering and was pleasantly surprised when I started seeing colors swirl behind my closed eyes. I first saw a soft pink color, which blended into a vivid purple-blue shade. These colors felt soothing and healing.*

*"When I finished my meditation and opened my eyes, I couldn't believe how crystal clear the meadow looked! It also felt like I was more a part of my surroundings, that I was somehow more connected. It was a marvelous feeling. I reflected on the messages I received and decided to heed the one about taking a break. The next day, I lined up a short retreat, even though it was during my preparation time for my case. Since this message from my inner voice came through so strongly, I decided to pay attention to it. Even with taking a few days off, it turned out that I still had plenty of time to do my research and compile my trial notes. I actually completed this step feeling more centered and focused than in the past.*

*"All in all, performing the nature meditation gave me a new perspective on what meditation can do for me and I know I'll now be more consistent with my daily, indoor sessions. As an added bonus, I certainly liked the renewed sparkle in my eyes and glow on my face as I looked at myself in the bathroom mirror when I arrived home. Is meditation an anti-aging device too?"*

## "Active" Meditations

Meditating does not always have to be a sedentary exercise. You can also perform an "active" meditation, which means going into a relaxed, receptive state while doing a repetitive motion, like walking, biking, swimming laps, or pulling weeds in your garden. All you have to do is repeat the same word or phrase (called a *mantra*) to yourself in a rhythmic way that matches the timing of the motion. As an example, when biking on a long, flat stretch of road, I like to tell myself, "I am expanding my consciousness" in a cadence that equals my pedaling speed.

Active meditations can be just as powerful as sedentary meditative postures. Speaking or chanting a mantra allows you to remain centered and grounded, while your psychic core becomes open to receiving information. Soon, the movement you are doing will become automatic as you go deeper within your psychic self. For both variety and spiritual growth, work movement-oriented meditations into your schedule. Vary them a bit to determine which types of activities, coupled with which mantras, produce your deepest receptive state.

## List of Strengths

This next exercise is a focused meditation done in increments, a little each day. It shows you how many wonderful, positive traits you possess and how some of these qualities can assist your psychic development. During your daily meditation over the course of one week, jot down in your journal three to four of your personal strengths. These strengths can include physical characteristics (beautiful eyes, strong body), physical talents (excellent swimmer, endurance runner), personality pluses (optimistic, intelligent), positive emotional makeup (even-keeled, compassionate), attitude toward other people and the world at large, etc.—the sky's the limit! No strength is too small to list. Have fun with this exercise and get comfortable with tooting your own horn. When completed, review your entire list to realize what you have to offer and how using these strengths can make you feel more empowered and integrated.

As a second step, pick out five of the strengths from your list that most catch your intuitive eyes. These top five strengths are those your psychic side wishes to expand upon. How can you utilize these strengths more on a daily basis? Pose this question to yourself during a meditation to help you determine effective and growth-oriented courses of action.

You may wish to continue adding to your list of strengths for the next couple of weeks. After you feel you have finished this exercise, copy or type this list, in columnar fashion, onto a single sheet of 8 ½" x 11" paper and then frame it. This plaque-like rendering will serve as a visual reminder of your unlimited capacity for growth.

I would like to close this chapter with another meditation script from one of my classes. The Rose Meditation is a wonderfully soothing narration; it helps to affirm how unique and multi-layered we are—and how ready we are to develop our psychic side. Record this one as well to play for yourself. Then periodically repeat this meditation to reinforce just how truly special you are and that you are well on the path to freeing up and integrating your intuition.

### Rose Meditation—Read Very Slowly—Time: 8–10 Minutes

Sit or recline comfortably…close your eyes…and ground yourself by sending out tree roots from the soles of your feet and the base of your spine…have these tree roots go through the floor and anchor them deeply into Mother Earth…slow your breath down and take very deep breaths, filling your lungs and torso completely…**[pause for 1.5 minutes]**…continue to relax…and gently release any thoughts about what happened earlier in the day or yesterday…gently release any thoughts about what you need to do later or tomorrow…release tension from any part of your body by sending your breath there…**[pause for 30 seconds]**…continue to relax, slowing the breath down…focus on feeling how your breath circulates throughout your body…**[pause for 1 minute]**…now in your mind's eye I want you to conjure up a beautiful rose bud…this rose bud is completely closed and you're simply gazing at it peacefully…**[pause for 10 seconds]**…note the color of the rose bud…note if there is a stem, if there are leaves, if there are thorns…what color is the stem?…what color are the leaves?…how many leaves and thorns are there?…focus again on the rose bud…you're continuing to gaze peacefully at this beautiful rose bud…**[pause for 10 seconds]**…and now as you're gazing at the rose bud, you notice a slight vibration…a slight movement…as you continue to gaze at the rose bud, you note <u>more</u> vibration and movement…**[pause for 10 seconds]**…and now the rose bud begins to open ever so slightly…you feel very peaceful waiting for the bud to open little by little…as it continues to slowly open, you can see more color and more of its petals and you note the shape of the petals…and now the rose bud is almost fully open…you can see the individual petals and how they are attached at the base of the bud…almost in a spiral formation…note any difference in the color of the petals…the rose is fully open now and you can see right down into the center of the flower…take in its full beauty…see how the petals are individual and yet interconnected with each other…and how the fully open flower sits on its stem…**[pause for 30 seconds]**…we are like the petals of the rose…we are made up of many different layers, all waiting to be uncovered…all individual layers, yet interconnected—making us a total, spiritually aware person…continue to gaze and marvel at the beauty and simplicity of this beautiful rose…taking it all in…**[pause for 1 minute]**…now take a super deep, cleansing breath…and take another super deep, cleansing breath…and take another super deep, cleansing breath and stretch your arms up and over your head…and you can open your eyes when you feel ready.

# 3

## *Trust Your Inner Self*

Now that you know how to meditate and have been practicing a bit, you are ready to perform the following two exercises. These exercises are designed to free up more of your intuitive voice. In addition, they focus on creating a smoother flow between your psychic side and the logical mind, which often tries to cast doubt about information received.

## Where Am I Now?

This first exercise is done in a written format and produces a current snapshot of your view of yourself and life in general. It also shows you how you regard various symbols that relate to psychic development, thus allowing you greater insight into how you can modify and recondition old thought patterns and attitudes. Your responses describing these symbols give you important feedback that will help you design ways to become more optimistic and intuitively empowered. After all, it is important to recognize any blocks we have that may cause delays in our spiritual evolution.

Be sure to give yourself enough time between each reply so that you can close your eyes and see in your mind's eye as much detail as possible. (Hint: record all of these details; they will aid you in your interpretation of the paragraphs.) Do not think too much before jotting down your answers—simply let your intuition bubble through and have fun!

## Paragraph #1

Ground yourself and take a few deep, cleansing breaths. In your mind's eye, place yourself on a road. There is a warm summer breeze and you are strolling down this road enjoying the day. Describe the road and its surroundings. *Close your eyes for a moment before writing.*

## Paragraph #2

You continue to walk down this road. You now see a key. Describe this key and describe what you do with it. *Close your eyes for a moment before writing.*

## Paragraph #3

You walk farther down this road. You now see a cup. Describe the cup's location in relation to the road and describe what the cup looks like. *Close your eyes for a moment before writing.*

## Paragraph #4

You walk farther down the road. You now come to a brook. You first describe the water in this brook and then describe if you walk into the brook, cross the brook, stay on the same side, or any other sort of interaction. *Close your eyes for a moment before writing.*

## Paragraph #5

You continue farther down the road, either on the same side or after you have crossed the brook. You now come to a wall. Describe the wall. *Close your eyes for a moment before writing.*

## Paragraph #6

Now interact with the wall by climbing it, sitting on it, or doing something else. Somehow, you get to a point where you can see beyond the wall. Describe your interaction with the wall. *Close your eyes for a moment before writing.*

And finally,

## Paragraph #7

Describe what you see beyond the wall. *Close your eyes for a moment before writing.*

Please turn to the Appendix for the meanings of the various symbols used in this exercise. After you look over the definitions of these symbols, reflect on your answers and what they signify. As you continue to work through this book, periodically review what you intuitively wrote, noting which aspects seem most important to your spiritual growth. As you expand your metaphysical knowledge base and get to know yourself more thoroughly, your written responses are likely to change over time.

*Paul, 44, had been a stockbroker for the past fifteen years. Up to now, his demanding career had been his highest priority. But like so many people in their forties, he began to take stock of his life and was now determined to free up and integrate more of his creative and intuitive sides into his day-to-day activities. I knew he would enjoy the Where Am I Now? homework assignment and would gain valuable information that would help him on his deepening psychic path. Here is what Paul wrote (the symbol prompts from the exercise are bolded):*

*"I am walking down a fairly wide dirt **road** that is lined with trees and low bushes. I can feel the warm summer breeze and can see sunlight filtering through the branches of the trees. Nobody else is around and I feel curious and expectant as I stroll down the road.*

"As I continue on my way, I see a bend in the road that curves slightly to the right. As I round the bend, I see a **key** in the middle of the road. I walk over to the key and stoop down to pick it up. It is a large, old skeleton key that looks worn and weathered. It is a faded gold color. The key feels good in my hand and I decide to put it in my left-hand pants pocket.

"I resume my walk and soon see a medium-sized boulder on the right side of the road. Sitting on top of this boulder is a **cup**. The cup is quite ornate and looks like a chalice. It is pewter with engravings all over it. The engravings are of an intricate design that seem to be some kind of ancient language. Besides the engravings, there are round jewels set into the pewter. These jewels are red and yellow. I notice the cup is empty.

"I walk farther down the road and can see the **brook** up ahead. The water in the brook is rushing very fast and is even splashing a little up onto the banks. I see small rocks and pebbles at the bottom of the brook. I decide to cool my feet, and I take off my socks and shoes. I then wade across the brook to the other side, stopping a few times to splash around and play.

"After I cross the brook and put on my socks and shoes, I continue on my way down the road. I look off to the left and can see a meadow through a break in the trees and low bushes. I turn off the road to explore the meadow. As I enter the meadow, I see that it is quite large and, roughly in the middle, a long **wall** cuts horizontally across the grass. This wall looks to be about seven feet high, and I can't see the meadow on the other side of it. I walk up to the wall and see that it is made up of very large stones set in a rather haphazard design. Kind of like those old stone walls you see in pictures of rural France or Ireland.

"I start to pull myself up with my arms so that I can sit on top of the wall. I'm not the best climber, so I kind of scramble up. Luckily it's not that high! The top of the wall is flat and about three feet wide. I sit down and rest, facing away from the road.

"Wow, what a view from up here! Little did I know what to expect **beyond the wall**. I see a huge expanse of land, with a whole village laid out in it. There are lots of trees, different types of medieval-looking houses, and even a castle far off in the distance. I also see many different animals *and birds, and a beautiful lake in the middle. This scene feels very lush, peaceful, and bountiful."*

To help Paul analyze his narrative, we dissected the exercise's primary components by reviewing the definitions of the various symbols (see Appendix). Here is what we uncovered about this stockbroker's inner workings (symbol prompts and interpretations are bolded):

Paul's **life path** is full of possibilities and growth, as evidenced by the wideness of his **road** and the fact that it is lined with living things (the trees and low bushes). He is also ready for new things to happen because there is a light source shining on his road (the filtered sunlight) and he feels "curious and expectant."

Paul appears ready to learn and absorb **knowledge** since his **key** is in plain view in the middle of the road—there is no way he can miss it. The fact that the key is an old design suggests that he has had prior lifetimes and may be able to tap into some of his accumulated wisdom from times past (see Chapter 10 on discovering past lives). The fact that Paul places the key in his left-hand pants pocket tells us he wishes to uncover emotional and intuitive knowledge.

Paul's current attitude regarding **understanding** appears to be action-oriented and directed toward understanding his role in the physical world (his **cup** is on the right side of the road). Similar to the key, the cup's ancient markings could indicate a past life that might hold important information for Paul to utilize in his current life. As an added bonus, the jewels set into the cup herald changes to occur in his first and third chakras (see colors commonly associated with the chakras in Chapter 5). Also, these colored jewels can be interpreted using Paul's personal definitions of red and yellow from his Color Log. The fact that the cup is empty signifies he is ready to gain more understanding about how he wishes to fit into his outer world.

Paul definitely has a healthy, vibrant attitude toward his **sexuality**. The fact that his **brook** has a strong current and that he interacts directly with the water ("splash around and play") indicates a person who is in *touch with his or her second chakra, which deals with sensuality and creativity.*

*Because Paul's **wall** is located in a meadow "off to the left" again brings up his desire to uncover more of his emotional and intuitive sides. His stone wall evokes themes of both sturdiness ("large stones") and randomness ("haphazard design"), which can mean that his approach to his **end of life, transition, and change** is solid, yet still being formed. In addition, Paul pulls himself up to sit on top of the wall and look out, which shows his determination to discover the nature of his transition after death.*

*And what does Paul see **beyond the wall**? His view of **eternity**—that which he'll experience after he concludes all of his human lifetimes—is full of optimism, nature, and community. It is interesting to note that here, again, we see a reference toward a time period from the past ("medieval-looking houses and even a castle"). Obviously, Paul is drawn to comfortable, peaceful environments. I pointed out to Paul that he can work on creating a similar atmosphere in his current life and that, by doing so, he would be enhancing his inner development. As a start, Paul added more plants and an indoor fountain to his condominium decor.*

*Performing this writing exercise gave Paul a great deal to think about and helped him to see where he is with his inner development. I suggested that he redo this homework assignment in three months; after completing the paragraphs a second time he will be able to gauge the progress of his ongoing growth.*

## Shower Yes/No Exercise

This next exercise is excellent for practicing how to trust your inner voice and prevent second-guessing. You know how relaxing and rejuvenating it is to walk along the water's edge on a beach or lakefront? Have you experienced inspirational thoughts or instantly come to a long-pondered decision by taking this type of stroll? The Shower Yes/No exercise's effectiveness is based on the same benefits derived from being in the proximity of negative water ions which are so soothing and get us to tap into our psychic side.

When you are standing under the shower's spray, pose a simple question to yourself in a form where the answer can only be either "Yes" or "No." It is best to start out with a question like, "Should I wear the blue shirt today?" or "Should I have chicken for dinner?" Silently ask yourself this question and whichever word bubbles up first, that is the answer sent from your intuitive self. Do not ask a second time. Now, you may think, "How can I get an answer so fast and so easily?" Trust your gut instinct. The goal here is for you to experience accessing a clear channel to your inner voice.

In the next day or two, progress to a tougher question like, "Should I accept the job offer with Company X?" or "Did I get everything off my chest when I spoke with Kim yesterday?" When you get an unobstructed "Yes" or "No" it is much easier to move forward with that person/decision/situation because you are not spinning your wheels and wasting valuable energy. Of course, with particularly difficult or complex decisions, using the Shower Yes/No exercise is helpful as an important adjunct to doing research and bouncing your ideas and feelings off of others. The key with this reconditioning exercise is that it allows us to practice implicitly believing our inner voices and, as a bonus, makes us feel stronger by fostering clarity.

# 4

## *External Energy: Auras*

### What is an Aura?

Auras are energy layers that surround all living things, including animals and plants. These layers are produced from our soul and correspond to our mental, emotional, and spiritual states of being. Learning how to see and feel auras can assist you in understanding your spiritual growth and can help you identify where you have energy blocks. Ever-changing, our auras are affected by our moods, external stimuli, and childhood experiences, just to name a few influences. Our auras also vary in strength as they project outward from our bodies. Sometimes they can appear as layers that outline the body and other times as sparks or elongated energy projectiles. In addition, auras can be seen as geometric shapes or washes of color floating in front of a person's face or torso. This often occurs because energy is malleable and alive.

### Aura Colors

Auras come in a wide array of colors. When first gaining experience in seeing auras, it is common to see them as a thin silhouette of gray or white around the body, especially the head and shoulders. Other colors will usually come into play as you practice and get more experienced. This is where your Color Log can come in handy; by knowing ahead of time what certain colors mean to you, you will have an easier time interpreting your own aura and those of others.

## Techniques for Seeing Auras

There are four main techniques for seeing auras. I encourage you to try all of the approaches to see which produces the most information. Be sure to have your journal and Color Log handy during your practice sessions so you can jot down any and all snippets. You can then reflect on these pieces of information and expand on them at your leisure.

So how should you practice? For reading your own aura, stand in front of a full-length mirror wearing solid, light-colored clothing. Make sure the wall behind you is free from pictures or distracting, patterned wallpaper. Always ground first and take some loop breaths. Then try the four methods outlined below. Keep track of how each one feels and record your experiences, including any colors and shapes you see.

### Aura Reading Techniques

- Make your eyes go unfocused and almost cross-eyed as you gaze at yourself, similar to seeing wavy lines rising above hot pavement.

- Gaze at your third eye (area between and slightly above your two physical eyes).

- Gaze at the quadrant between your head and shoulder.

- Gaze at yourself, then slowly close your eyelids. You will most likely see an outline of yourself on the backs of your lids.

*Gloria, 35, a stay-at-home mother of two young children, felt like she was losing her identity. Her daughters kept her extremely busy and she rarely had time to meditate or work on exercises from our class. Intent on encouraging her to focus on her self-growth, I asked her to carve out a little time to practice the aura self-reading techniques. Even though she had mentioned in some of our class sessions that her prior attempts at seeing her own aura did not work, I felt these particular methods would produce results for her and make her feel more empowered. She came over one afternoon so I could help her practice.*

When we set up the private lesson, I told Gloria to wear plain, light-colored clothing. This would lessen any visual distractions. She arrived in a casual, monotone outfit: a cream T-shirt and beige slacks. Earlier in the day, I removed the painting from the wall opposite my large bathroom mirror, as this was to be Gloria's practice site. I also adjusted the lighting so it would be slightly softer for her as she gazed at her reflection.

Standing in front of the mirror, Gloria started by closing her eyes, slowing her breath, and then visualizing and sending out tree roots in order to ground herself. I could feel her determination as her face and body posture became more relaxed. When she told me she was ready, I briefly went over the four aura reading styles and reminded her not to put any pressure on herself. Rather, she should imagine herself as a calmly flowing river as she moved from one technique to another.

I asked Gloria to slowly open her eyes and try the first method: unfocused eyes. I also requested she say aloud anything she was seeing and feeling so that I could jot down her remarks for her journal. Gloria first reported she felt heat coming off her body and that her reflection looked grayish and fuzzy as she gazed at herself with her eyes almost crossed. I told her this was her core energy she was feeling and that she was starting to let her physical body be less visually prominent. Gloria gazed at herself in this manner for about two minutes, continuing to take deep breaths.

I next asked her to bring her eyes back into focus and look directly at her third eye. As she did so, I could see her relax even further and I could tell she was feeling more centered. She told me that as she looked at her sixth chakra (which is the third eye—see Chapter 5), the rest of her body became detectable through her peripheral vision, and then she saw a thin layer of grayish-white outlining her head and shoulders. I asked Gloria to take a few deep breaths to see if this outline intensified or extended further down her body. She said she could see the outline a bit more, but it did not spread to other areas. I told Gloria she was seeing her first aura, and that one's aura does not always have to be colorful.

Moving to the third technique, Gloria began to gaze at the quadrant between her head and right shoulder. She intuitively chose her right side; I *told her that either side usually produces similar results. I reminded her to keep taking deep breaths and, as she did so, she reported seeing a wash of green-blue color over her face and upper body. Gloria laughed with excitement and I put a star by the color so she could later look up its meaning in her Color Log. She said she liked seeing her aura in this way, and I asked her if viewing her aura helped confirm that she is a dynamic, energetic being. Gloria replied that it made her think about her personal power.*

*We next tried the last aura-reading method: gazing first into the mirror and then slowly closing the eyelids. Gloria smiled broadly when she first closed her eyes, saying an outline of her body popped through very fast, and that all around her body was a layer of the same green-blue color. She also reported a few long, slender projectiles coming out of her head and left hand. These projectiles were bright orange. For future interpretation, I jotted down these colors. The fact she saw so much of her aura when executing this technique told us that, for now, this was her aura reading method of choice.*

*After she finished, Gloria commented she did not expect to see so much of her aura, and that it made her feel more alive and in touch with her true identity—a colorful, questing woman. The energy projectiles were especially significant and told her she still has a very active mind and is in the process of activating her intuition, as evidenced by the left-hand aura burst. This exercise was quite life affirming for her and helped to boost her confidence. In other words, she saw that it <u>was</u> possible to develop her inner self while still being an available mother to her two daughters. Gloria simply needed proof she was making progress and, in the meantime, was reminded of the importance of giving herself time for self-exploration.*

If at first you find yourself experiencing difficulty seeing your aura, review the checklist below. Often, giving yourself enough preparation time can serve as the needed catalyst for freeing up more of your intuitive eyes.

### Aura Reading Checklist

- How is your breathing? Closing your eyes for a moment and focusing on taking deep breaths can help activate your psychic message center.

- Are you truly grounded? Having a stable anchor into Mother Earth allows your intuitive side the freedom to be very receptive.

- Are you tired or under the weather? Stop for now and try another day when you are feeling stronger.

- Are you trying too hard? Slow down and be gentle with yourself—after all, this is simply practice, and you are working at your own pace.

You can also try reading a friend's aura by having your partner stand in front of a neutral-colored, blank wall. Then go through the four techniques, being sure to have your journal nearby to record snippets of information. Animals can be good subjects as well—as long as they are sitting or lying peacefully. When I first practiced reading auras, I would hike out into the woods, sit on a ridge, and gaze at a line of trees on an opposite mountain top. By looking at a whole row of majestic pines, I soon could see which ones projected more energy. This was a wonderful way to develop my skill and helped me gain confidence when I read friends and, later, clients.

## Feeling Auras

Auras can be felt too. Since one of our five psychic senses involves touch, it is beneficial to learn how to feel auras. To do this, you need another person. Begin by positioning a friend or colleague across the room. Have that person stand relaxed and with their eyes closed. Your partner then starts to visualize sending his or her energy toward you, perhaps for about two minutes. Close your eyes, ground yourself, and take deep breaths as you focus on your assistant. Next, tell your partner you are ready and slowly walk toward your subject, with your arms out in front of you and your palms facing his or her body. Do not have too much space between yourself and your friend, as it is then too easy to walk crookedly. While continuing to send energy, your partner should open their eyes right after you begin walking. By doing so, you can be gently voice-guided back onto a fairly straight path if you start to veer.

Stop walking as soon as you begin to feel your subject's energy. You may feel a pillow-like texture or a hot or cold sensation. Before taking a few steps closer, bend down slightly and feel around in the lower region. Then reach up to feel the empty space in front of your partner's chest, shoulders, and head. You may feel differences in his or her energy in these areas. Also, note where the person's energy feels strongest: is it the right or left side? Take a few, deep breaths and focus a few more minutes on feeling energy. With your eyes closed, you may see colors, images, or hear a word or phrase. Now take a couple more steps and repeat the feeling process.

After a few additional minutes, open your eyes and, in your journal, record all you experienced. Be sure to ask your friend to tell you how far away you were when you first detected his or her aura. Then discuss your findings with your subject and get feedback. Include definitions of any colors you saw. Do not become discouraged if your assistant only verifies a couple of things you encountered. You are simply practicing, and at this point you do not have to be concerned with accuracy. This exercise allows you to concentrate on trusting your intuition and teaches you not to second-guess yourself with the logical mind.

# 5

# *Internal Energy: Chakras*

Now, we are going to dig a bit deeper into our psychic core and learn about our internal energy centers. Understanding and working with chakras permit us to get to the heart of how we tick, which in turn can help us see how to grow into a fully integrated, spiritual person.

## What are Chakras?

The word "chakra" (pronounced *sháh-krah*) comes from the ancient Sanskrit language and means "wheel." Wheel is certainly appropriate, as our chakras correspond to atoms which are made up of energy and spin in a circular fashion—just like a spinning wheel. We have seven primary chakras that start at the base of our spine, run up our backbone, and end at the top of our head. They are three-dimensional and can be accessed from both the front and back of our bodies. Most importantly, almost all of the chakras relate directly to our emotions. Because of this, energy in these centers can become blocked or sluggish, depending on what we are processing—or not processing.

Listed below are the seven chakras, their definitions, locations in the body, and colors commonly associated with them. They are numbered from the ground up to reflect how important it is to pull energy from Mother Earth, have her rejuvenating and cleansing properties pass through our chakras, and then flow out of our heads and toward the heavens.

## First Chakra—Survival

Definition: Emotions dealing with shelter, food, money, and surviving in the outside world.
Location: The base of the spine, at the coccyx.
Color: Red.

## Second Chakra—Sexuality

Definition: Emotions dealing with sex, love partners, artistic creativity, fathers, and father figures.
Location: For women, in line with the uterus; for men, midway between the penis and the navel.
Color: Orange.

## Third Chakra—Fears and Risks

Definition: Emotions about pushing past old fears and attitudes; getting comfortable with taking risks.
Location: The solar plexus. To locate, place the outside of one of your pinky fingers lengthwise across the top of your navel. Have your other three fingers parallel to your pinky. At the top edge of your four fingers is your solar plexus. If you press a finger firmly into your torso in this spot, you will feel uncomfortable. This is because the greatest number of nerve endings is found in the solar plexus.
Color: Yellow.

## Fourth Chakra—Universal Love/Self-Love

Definition: Emotions dealing with loving yourself, others, and the global community; learning to open up the heart center.
Location: The heart.
Color: Green.

## Fifth Chakra—Communication

Definition: Emotions dealing with speaking your truth; expressing yourself both verbally and through the written word.
Location: The throat.
Color: Blue.

The next two chakras are quite esoteric in nature—as opposed to incorporating a specific emotion—and deal more directly with your psychicness and accessing the deepest levels of your intuition. Note that the colors for these chakras are both in the purple family, as purple is commonly equated with higher spiritual knowledge.

## Sixth Chakra—Seeing

Definition: Utilizing your intuitive abilities to receive important messages for yourself and others.
Location: The third eye (area between and slightly above your two eyes).
Color: Indigo.

## Seventh Chakra—Knowing

Definition: Utilizing your intuitive abilities to link directly with the Universal Energies, your higher self, and any assisting spiritual guides.
Location: The crown of the head.
Color: Lavender.

It is interesting to point out that the colors of chakras one through six mirror the order of the colors in a rainbow or in a beam of light as it refracts through a prism. Since we are all made up of energy, including our chakras, it makes sense that the chakra colors would follow that of basic physics and correspond to the energetic color pattern found in simple, natural occurrences. The color of the seventh chakra combines white with purple to create lavender. Because white is often associated with complete spiritual enlightenment, it begins to be incorporated into this top chakra, which is the closest to the more esoteric and advanced energies that reside in the heavens.

Locate each of the seven primary chakras on your body to familiarize yourself with them. Next, try a meditation where you focus on feeling each chakra and the type of energy each one contains. Record your findings in your journal so that you can see the difference in energy flow, colors, and overall sensations. Afterward, close your eyes again, take a couple of deep breaths, and ask your inner voice which chakra or chakras need the most attention at this point in time. Record your answer. Over the next few days, reflect on this response, and think of ways you can make the energy move more smoothly through this chakra or chakras. In general, learning about your chakras will help you with other types of exercises that focus on the total well-being of your core essence.

*Don, 28, was a young man who had just finished graduate school. He had a brand new M.S. in Psychology and was eager to begin his career of helping people to better understand themselves. However, having grown up with parents who were former hippies, he didn't want to approach his field in a routine, clinical way. His mother and father had taught him the importance of acknowledging and integrating the entire self from an intellectual, emotional, and spiritual standpoint. He wanted to instill a similar philosophy in his future patients. Don soaked up our class discussions about the chakras and I knew he would gain a great deal of valuable experience by performing the basic Chakra Meditation. Perhaps, as part of their treatment plan, he eventually could teach his patients how to assess their own chakras.*

*He began by lying face up on his bed, with pillows under his head and behind his knees. First, he closed his eyes, sent out tree roots, and brought down his sacred star so he would stay grounded during the exercise. Don next slowed his breath and began loop breathing. Concentrating on his first chakra, he reached underneath himself and placed a hand at the base of his* spine. In his mind's eye, he saw this chakra as a small, round, slightly vibrating object. Don took this movement to mean that energy was flowing through the chakra. Its small size felt rather vulnerable, which struck him as an accurate representation of his current, tentative view about his new career. At this point, Don was not exactly sure how he wanted to let the outside world know he was an available counselor.

He moved his hand to his lower abdomen so it was on top of his second chakra and concentrated on this center. Instead of getting a visual image, Don felt a bit of heat and some tenderness as he gently pressed down. He heard the phrase, "Free up your creativity" from his inner voice. He promised himself to focus on this direct message in the coming days and he felt eager to brainstorm ways he could accomplish this self-given command.

When Don progressed to his third chakra, he immediately saw a blooming yellow-orange rose. He thought for a moment about what this color combination signified for him. In his mind's eye, this rose radiated a strong life force. It felt very positive and growth-oriented. Don noted that this chakra had lots of energy flowing through it and decided that this meant he must be ready to take some new risks.

He continued up the chakra ladder to the fourth chakra, directly over his physical heart. When he placed his hand over this area, he felt some sadness and received a mental picture of a thick tangle of weeds. These weeds felt quite old and Don couldn't see any light filtering through them. He took this to mean that his energy was blocked as it tried to pass through this chakra and the blockage was due to upsetting heartfelt experiences from his past. After he finished the meditation, he would try to figure out which events caused this obstruction.

Don's hand over his fifth chakra divulged a pulsating effect and in his mind's eye he saw a large pool of water, similar to a lake. This chakra felt very energetic and he didn't detect any blockages in it. Knowing that this center deals with communication, Don told himself that he must be getting his ideas across to others in a healthy and direct way.

By the time Don was ready to send his inner focus to his sixth chakra, he was getting a good idea about how different the chakras can look and feel.

*The manner in which he was pulling life-force energy from Mother Earth certainly became apparent once he concentrated on the state of his chakras. With a few fingers over his third eye, he felt a bit of heat again and saw a diamond-like shape. After taking a few deep breaths, he could tell that this diamond was an actual crystal, and that he could send out his psychic energy through this object. He felt very expansive with this visualization and it helped to confirm his determination to be an integrated being.*

*Don's seventh chakra, at the crown of his head, appeared milky and swirling in his mind's eye, and he was pleased to note its movement. He liked the philosophy about this chakra, especially the fact that it connects to one's higher self and the Universal Energies. He interpreted the movement to be indicative of his desire to incorporate the more otherworldly realms.*

*Remembering our class homework assignment, Don next reviewed his chakra findings and decided that chakras one, two, and four seemed to need the most assistance. He told himself he would focus on these three centers to get their energy more clean-flowing and harmonious with the rest of his inner layers. As a start, in his next meditation he would send specific colors to these chakras—colors that would help them energize and heal.*

## Chakra Conditioning Chant

Periodically conditioning your chakras helps to keep their energy healthy and flowing unimpeded through your body. The vibrations from this particular chanting exercise resonate deep within the chakras, helping to energize our entire bodies as well. The phrase we are chanting is an affirming, empowering statement: "Live Very Richly You Happy One." But, instead of chanting this statement in its entirety, we instead attach the first letter of each word to the sound "um," and repeat this syllable three times as we focus on moving up the chakra ladder, from one through six (we treat the seventh chakra a bit differently, which is explained below). For instance, for the first chakra we chant, "Lum, Lum, Lum", for the second chakra we chant, "Vum, Vum, Vum", and so on. For the sixth chakra, since its word in the phrase begins with a vowel, try chanting "Ohm" to draw the sound out a bit. I like to vary the tones of my chant and loosely go up the musical scale with each chakra syllable.

Do not rush through this chant. Ground yourself first, take some deep, loop breaths, close your eyes, and then begin. Chant as loudly as you wish to feel more vibrational reverberations. At the seventh chakra, there is no actual syllable to chant; instead, at this chakra we remain silent and visualize our energy continuing to rise upward, flowing from the top of our head and connecting with the heavens. As an alternative, you can also condition your chakras by visualizing them radiating the color most commonly associated with them.

## Scanning Chakras for Cords

We constantly send out energy toward others. Whether we are having a business meeting with a colleague or client, arguing with a family member or friend, laughing with a child, or making love with our partner, we are directing energy to that person. This energy, whether positive or challenging, flows out of one or more of our chakras into one or more of the chakras of the person with whom we are interacting. The flow of energy from one individual to another is referred to as a chakra "cord." Just like a cord we use to tie two items together, chakra cords bind us to other people. Obviously, having numerous cords flowing out of our chakras into others can be a confusing and overwhelming energetic experience! We may not always feel these cords, but over time they deplete our energy and can contribute to fatigue, irritability, and chakra energy blockages.

It is important to occasionally scan our chakras to check for cords. This takes a bit of practice, but can be incorporated into three or four of your meditations each week. During such sessions, close your eyes, ground yourself, and begin your loop breathing. Then, one by one, gently send your inner focus to each chakra, beginning with number one. Allow yourself to experience this chakra and try to assess if you feel any cords coming out of it. You may receive an image of, or get a sense of, a rope, a string, or a mass-like structure. In your mind's eye, you can then ceremoniously cut this cord with a special pair of sacred shears or a ritual knife. Or you can visualize yourself pulling the cord (or similar substance) out of this chakra. Then move up the chakra ladder to the second chakra and repeat the process. You do not have to scan all seven chakras during the same meditation, but try to complete them within two consecutive days. Often, chakra cords can be quite deep and stubborn and can sometimes immediately grow back upon removal. Such cords are usually formed in childhood and we simply have been carrying them around with us into our adult years.

When we scan our chakras for cords, we can also send a specific color to help them heal, unblock, and rejuvenate. After you remove cords, visualize a particular color flowing into that chakra (review your Color Log if necessary). Whichever color feels appropriate is the correct color to send; it does not have to be the color commonly associated with that energy center. Anything we do to help our chakras become more balanced helps balance our entire selves and assists greatly in achieving total integration of body, mind, and spirit.

Keep track of your findings during your chakra cord scanning sessions. For each chakra, note if you perceived a cord, how you severed this cord, and what color you sent to the chakra. Remember that even our most positive and fulfilling interactions with people produce cords that we need to periodically remove. Spiritual work and personal growth are very individualistic; we want our core energy to stay somewhat separate so we can use it for our ongoing life-path work.

Chakra energy work is a rather advanced technique and it may take a little while to feel or see your chakras and any cords embedded in them. If you initially find yourself having difficulty receiving information, try the following:

- Review where each chakra is located and what it stands for.

- Slow down the pace of the exercises and only focus on two adjacent chakras per meditative or cord scanning session.

- Remind yourself that these skills will become easier with practice and time. After all, you are doing deep work and are exercising your fledgling psychic muscle!

# 6

## *Protecting Your Psychic Energy*

Besides cutting chakra cords, there are other ways to keep your energy separate from the energy of others. As you are no doubt opening up your psychic self by practicing a schedule of regular meditations and performing the exercises and techniques presented thus far, you may be experiencing feelings of extra sensitivity. Have you been picking up more often on others' moods? Have you been undergoing an increase in extrasensory perception (ESP) occurrences, like knowing when the phone will ring or receiving premonitory dreams? Such happenings are common and are an indication that you possess a more consistent pathway to your psychic side. However, as stated earlier, these types of events can feel quite overwhelming and can cause sleeplessness and fatigue.

At times, it becomes necessary to apply various techniques to keep ourselves from being energy-depleted while we are developing our intuitive side. We do not want to operate in a totally open psychic manner with the outside world. Even if your ultimate goal is to become a metaphysical practitioner, you need to know how not to absorb your clients' energy. I have listed below four helpful safeguards that allow you to interact with friends, colleagues, partners, and clients without feeling drained in the process (or afterward). Each exercise is extremely simple, but you will be pleasantly surprised at each one's effectiveness.

# #1 Coat of Mirrors

When dealing with someone on the phone, or face-to-face, where negativity or extreme emotionality may be involved, try this technique. In your mind's eye, imagine yourself putting on a coat that is made of mirrors. These mirrors all face outward, toward the other person. By facing away from you, the mirrors simply deflect all unwanted energy so that you do not absorb any of it. You can even add mirrored boots, gloves, hat, or mask to your ensemble. Since I resonate with the shape of circles, my gear is made up of round, interlocking mirrors. Be as creative as you like. This exercise is quite positive and powerful, as you are not wishing any ill will toward the other person, but are simply choosing not to take in any of his or her energy. I have used my Coat of Mirrors with troublesome family members, argumentative employers, and problematic clients. Your Coat of Mirrors allows you to stay balanced and truly present in the midst of difficult interactions.

*Martha, 50, was a waitress and the divorced mother of a teenaged son. She was having a hard time with her son's fluctuating moods and ever-increasing heated arguments. She did not always have enough time or energy to devote to him and she wanted to interact with less intensity. Martha's main objective was to learn how not to absorb her son's out-of-control feelings, which in turn caused her to lash out at him. I knew the Coat of Mirrors exercise would assist her on this mission.*

*To determine what her coat looked like, Martha did a short meditation late one morning before going in for her shift at the restaurant. She sat quietly, grounded, and began her loop breathing. She then conjured up an image of herself in her mind's eye and concentrated on visualizing her mirrored apparel. Much to her delight, Martha almost instantly saw results. She thought, "I really must need to use this technique." Her coat consisted of a full-length garment made up of triangular-shaped mirrors. All of the mirrors, of course, faced outward. She even saw mirrored boots peeking out from beneath the coat and decided to add a derby-shaped hat to put on her head. Martha's Coat of Mirrors, with its accompanying reflective accessories, felt protective and nurturing.*

*At the next class session, Martha reported that her meditation to discover her personal Coat of Mirrors came none too soon. She ended up utilizing this technique for the first time soon after she arrived home that very evening. Typically exhausted from serving demanding customers, she longed for a peaceful stretch of time before retiring. However, her son had other plans and insisted on confronting her as soon as she walked through the front door.*

*"Why did you clean up my room?" he yelled. "I don't want you looking through my things!"*

*"I just—" Martha began, then stopped herself. Before she continued, she quickly donned her Coat of Mirrors, hat, and boots. Now she felt she could talk to her son without spiraling with him into a screaming match. His anger would simply be reflected back to him, and she would avoid absorbing his sour mood.*

*"I wanted to help you organize your paperwork because you told me last week you had a hard time finding research material for your English assignment. I wasn't snooping."*

*"But, Mom, I have my own way of doing things. I don't like to work in a clean environment," he protested. "It's too anal."*

*Martha's mirrored apparel was working: she didn't feel nearly as defensive, nor did she feel like she had to justify her actions. In fact, she could be more objective and somewhat removed as her son expressed himself. As a bonus she did not expect, she actually felt more compassionate and understanding.*

*"OK, I hear you," Martha replied. "I won't do it again."*

*In the subsequent weeks, Martha utilized her Coat of Mirrors many more times, both at the beginning of other potential arguments with her teenager and at work when she had to deal with disrespectful customers. Little by little, Martha felt the benefits of this energy-protecting exercise, which included less fatigue and irritability, and a greater tolerance of others' less-than-ideal personalities. She soon thought of myriad additional sit-*

*uations where her mirrors would allow her to successfully interact with difficult or emotionally charged people.*

## #2 Begone Statement

Since I believe in reincarnation, this next exercise helps me feel connected to my former life during the Middle Ages when I was a healer and herbalist. I also believe many of you were present during this same time period; if you were not, the word we utilize in this technique can still be of benefit because of its popular and effective use during ancient group rituals.

Whenever you are feeling overwhelmed or bombarded with negative thinking caused by other people's or society's unrealistic expectations or demands upon you, take a few deep breaths and say to yourself, "Begone!" This ceremonial word, primarily used in centuries past, targets that negative part of ourselves—the part that causes us to lose confidence in our abilities or to take on too much of another's energy. No matter how often you need to say "Begone!" it will always be a helpful reconditioning tool for abruptly nipping away unconstructive or unproductive thoughts.

## #3 White Light

Remember the grounding method of gently encasing yourself in a star's white rays (refer to Chapter 2)? Using white light can also efficiently protect your psychic self. Whenever you wish not to absorb another person's energy (whether you are interacting by phone or in person) visualize putting a white light around yourself, your house, your car, and anything else you wish to safeguard. This white light can instantly materialize in your mind's eye or you can imagine a star and its healing white rays. Similar to the Coat of Mirrors, the White Light technique is meant to keep your energy clear of unwanted influences without hurting or impeding anyone in the process.

## #4 Sea Salt Shower

As stated in Chapter 1, using sea salt as an economical cleansing and grounding agent can help tremendously in removing other people's energies. If you have a particularly trying interaction with someone, take a full-body sea salt shower. Bring a plastic container of sea salt into the shower stall with you. Before you turn on the water, gently rub the salt all over your body, including the top of your head so that you cleanse your crown chakra too. Then turn on the shower and rinse. You will emerge totally refreshed and your core energy will again be 100 percent your own.

To assist you with keeping track of your experiences with these psychic protection techniques, feel free to use the prompts below as you jot down your findings.

### Psychic Protection Techniques

- Coat of Mirrors
  Date? Reason used? Type of mirrored clothing? Results achieved?

- Begone Statement
  Date? Trying to dispel what negative-based statements? Results achieved?

- White Light
  Date? Put white light around whom/what? Purpose(s)? Results achieved?

- Sea Salt Shower
  Date? Purpose? Results achieved?

## Spiritual Ethics

Having presented the above approaches to psychic protection, what do you do if you, nonetheless, receive an important intuitive message or dream about someone that you feel needs to be expressed? There is a code of ethics involved with relaying psychic impressions. It is not

appropriate to automatically tell somebody a piece of personal information about him or herself that you received during a meditation,
dream, or in your normal waking state. Rather, it is always best to first
ask that person's permission. You cannot assume people want to hear
such information; after all, it may scare them or they might be shocked
that you picked up on something they thought was well hidden inside
themselves. If you cannot get permission, a helpful alternative is to
send positive energy in a general manner toward that person to wish
them well and to wish them continued self-reflection so they can hear
their own inner voice.

# 7

# *Crystal Energies: Spiritual &*
# *Practical*

Crystals are wonderful tools that amplify and transmit energy and can be thought of as magical batteries. Whatever you are trying to open up and release within yourself, using crystals in your techniques and rituals can accelerate the process. They have an otherworldly energy as well, and many people believe their properties are affected by the planets and stars.

On a spiritual level, crystals aid us in our psychic development in the areas of balance, growth, and transitions to new levels of awareness. On a practical level, crystals assist in enhancing the atmosphere of our home or office, help to provide restful sleep patterns, improve our constitutional health, and promote clarity in our thinking.

## Basic Crystal Properties

Crystals fall into two main property types: projective and receptive. As human beings, we also contain both projective and receptive traits (i.e., giving and receiving), and can work with crystals to achieve more of a balance between these two qualities.

Projective crystals contain attributes that deal with aggressiveness, courage and determination, attracting luck and success, and interacting with the outside world. Receptive crystal attributes foster psychic awareness and grounding and can attract healing, money, and love.

## Crystal Color Associations

So, how do we determine which stones are projective and which are receptive? Primarily by their color. We already know the overall, symbolic importance of color (remember your Color Log?). In order to give you an idea of the variety of ways this tool can be used, listed below are ten crystal colors and qualities commonly ascribed to them.

Purple: Receptive. Highly spiritual; relieves depression, promotes physical healing, and helps with mental illness.

Orange: Projective. Focuses on personal power, helps with low self-esteem, and can be a symbol of success.

Pink: Receptive. Encourages calming, soothing, self-love vibrations; increases feelings of peace and happiness.

Yellow: Projective. Enhances communication (both writing and speaking) and is good for safe travel; also encourages healthy digestion.

Red: Projective. Promotes willpower and courage; strengthens the physical body.

Blue: Receptive. Fosters peace, calms emotions, and reduces fears; helps alleviate pains from the body.

Green: Receptive. Strengthens overall health and promotes physical healing. Also good for grounding and can enhance fertility in people and plants.

Black: Receptive. Fosters self-control, quiet power, and grounding.

White: Receptive. Encourages sleep and increased psychicness.

Multi-colored: Both projective and receptive. Since such crystals contain multiple colors, their uses are a combination of the colors you see (e.g., opals and tourmalines).

## Crystal Shapes

The shapes of stones also play a role when you consider what crystals to use. Listed below are ten common crystal shapes and their meanings.

Heart-shaped: Stimulates or draws love—both on the giving and receiving levels.

Round: Symbolizes the feminine and helps with love and attraction.

Square: Symbolizes the Earth, prosperity, abundance, and grounding.

Thin/long: Symbolizes the masculine and helps to direct energy toward a goal.

Body part shape: Strengthens that particular organ, limb, or physical feature.

Egg-shaped: Stimulates creativity and fresh ideas; also good for fertility.

Diamond: Attracts riches.

Triangular: Helps with protection of self and home.

Pyramid: Directs intentions because you can visualize your desired goal being released through its tip.

L-shaped: Assists with attracting good fortune.

## Choosing a Crystal

Good places to purchase crystals include metaphysical shops and bookstores, psychic fairs, and gem shows. It is best to choose specimens by what attracts you; for instance, color, shape, and size. When shopping for crystals, you may feel flushed when you look at them or feel heat as you hold them. This is the stone's energy that you are experiencing. Try holding crystals in your left hand first, since this is our psychic and receptive side. Most importantly, take your time and listen to your inner voice so that you choose the appropriate ones. Some people feel there is a difference between raw versus polished pieces, but this difference is usually negligible and one form is not necessarily more powerful than the other.

## Working with Your Crystals

Initially, get comfortable with your new tools. Try carrying them around in your left and right pockets, depending on how you want to enhance or accelerate the qualities associated with each side of the body (refer to discussion in Chapter 1). You can also put them inside your pillowcase at night and sleep with them. A third—and very popular—method of interacting with your crystals is to suspend them on a chain or cord and wear them as a pendant near or over a chakra; for example, over your throat or heart center. Taking this idea one step further, you can also tape, or tie with cloth, stones onto your body underneath your clothes (women can put them inside their bras too).

Two easy exercises to practice with your crystals include the following:

- Sit quietly with one of your crystals and direct into it any negative or counterproductive thoughts you wish to release. Visualize in your mind's eye these pessimistic feelings flowing out of you and into the stone. Alternatively, you can direct a positive intention into the specimen, such as the desired outcome of a goal or decision. This is called "programming" a crystal. Programming a stone often includes repeating a chant or affirmative statement while placing your intention; e.g., "I will secure new employment in a field I enjoy."

  Working with a crystal to help dispel negative energy, or to accelerate achievement of a goal, is done on a daily basis. Once the targeted result is obtained, the crystal used in this modality is cleansed (see discussion later in this chapter on cleansing crystals).

- Place four to six crystals of similar size into a pouch and, without looking, pick one from the container. The stone you choose mirrors the current atmosphere you are in. Reflect on the crystal chosen to uncover any messages from your inner voice about how its properties encourage your psychic development. In a week or so, try performing this exercise again, only this time substitute a couple of the original crystals with different ones. It is interesting to note if the same crystal appears a second time, or if you need to now focus on a different aspect of your inner growth. This exercise is similar to a divination method used with Rune stones, an ancient Celtic oracle.

# Meditating with Crystals

As mentioned earlier, crystals are amplifiers of intention. This becomes most apparent when incorporating crystals into your meditations. Basically, there are four postures to try with the stones. These positions include:

- Holding a crystal in your left hand to more deeply access your psychic and receptive side.

- Holding a crystal against your heart to open up your heart center and open yourself to more nurturing and loving feelings.

- Holding a crystal against your third eye to increase intuition and connection to your inner voice and higher self.

- Laying down and placing one or more crystals over one or more of your chakras to assist with unblocking and balancing them.

When meditating with your stones, be sure to record any and all images, colors, and words. Messages received from our crystal companions can be quite impacting and thought provoking!

*Sylvia, 64, was a retired, middle-school, art teacher who wanted to devote the rest of her career to mastering a new artistic style. In the past, her forte had been realistic watercolor landscapes and portraits. She eventually wanted to hire an agent to market her new pieces to galleries. However, her recent attempts at activating her inspiration produced nothing concrete. She was becoming increasingly frustrated and secretly wondered if her creative juices had dried up during her years of teaching preteens the basics of the color wheel and how to achieve a three-dimensional effect with charcoal.*

*Being an extremely visual artist, Sylvia enjoyed our class discussions about crystals and their healing properties. She appreciated their natural beauty and loved looking at the stones' colorful, varied hues and feeling their smooth surfaces. I encouraged her to start collecting crystals and experiment with how they could help uncover another layer of her creative self.*

*After purchasing a beautiful amethyst and lovely rose quartz, Sylvia decided to try meditating with them.*

*Late one evening, she took out her two new crystals and sat with her feet up in her comfortable recliner. She grounded herself and began to peacefully gaze at the deep purple and medium pink stones in her hands. They began to warm from her body heat and she could feel their aliveness. In order to help activate her psychic side, Sylvia placed the rose quartz in her lap and, closing her eyes, held the amethyst in her left hand. As she focused, she soon received an image of herself lounging against several large pillows covered in a rich tapestry fabric. This material felt wonderful and was comprised of various earth tones. The pillows enveloped her gently. She wasn't sure about the symbolism of this scene, but tucked it away in her memory for recording into her journal later.*

*Sylvia next took the rose quartz in her left hand and, still with her eyes closed, took several deep breaths and asked her inner voice for a message. She waited quietly for a few moments and then began to see a swirling pink light. Sylvia distinctly heard the phrase, "Visit the crystal cave" and, as she concentrated more deeply, found herself inside just such a cavern. This place was full of different sized crystals growing from the walls, ceiling, and even the floor of the cave. Each stone reflected a rainbow of colors. In all her life, Sylvia had never felt so much energy. She thought to herself that here was a place she could come to during meditations, not only to replenish her own energy reservoir, but also to help release more of her creativity.*

*Wanting to try one more meditative posture, Sylvia placed the rose quartz back in her lap and held the amethyst against her third eye. She again centered herself and gently closed her eyes. When she held the crystal against this chakra, she felt a slight buzzing and then, in her mind's eye, saw herself standing in front of an eight-foot tall canvas. On this canvas was a lovely, abstract collage made up of pieces of fabric, beautifully woven rope fragments, and other three-dimensional items. In her heart, Sylvia knew she had created this art piece. So that's why I saw those tapestry pillows! she thought. The canvas looked like a giant multi-media creation.*

*Sylvia concluded her meditation and released a cleansing sigh. She certainly had received her answer as to what genre she should now work within: her inner voice had sent her a very clear message to become a textural artist and design huge bodies of work. Her crystals had succeeded in guiding her to a deeper creative layer within herself and she felt ready to explore this new modality. It seemed to make sense, too, for Sylvia had always been a tactile person and loved to touch things; it just never occurred to her to incorporate this personality trait into her art.*

You can also meditate with crystal imagery. Remember the chakra scanning and cord cutting exercise (see Chapter 5)? Instead of, or in addition to, sending a particular color to a chakra, you may find it helpful during meditations to visualize placing a small crystal inside the chakra. This crystal can assist in soothing, healing, and protecting that chakra from the type of cords that tend to deeply imbed themselves or from emotional wounds that can cause energy to become blocked.

Lastly, do not forget to take a crystal or two with you when you meditate outdoors. Doing so can help accelerate the deepening process and free up more psychic and symbolic messages.

## Cleansing Your Crystals

It is important to periodically clean your crystals. Since they are transmitters of energy, stones need to be cleared after they have been used for a particular purpose (like sending a negative thought into them or for programming), when they are used in connection with a specific chakra, or simply when they are touched often by other people. We do not want our crystals to become clouded with built-up energy from prior uses or outside stimuli. In fact, stones will oftentimes show us when they need to be cleansed: you may see cracks or dark spots inside them that represent a particularly deep work session. To clean, there are many different methods. All of the techniques listed below incorporate a natural element.

## Crystal Cleaning Methods

- *Water*: Dissolve a small amount of sea salt in a dish of water (you can also use ocean water). Place crystals in the dish for forty-eight hours. Note: you may need to leave the crystals in the water for a longer length of time if they do not appear cleared. Then remove and dry the stones. Alternatively, if you live by or are camping near a river, you can place crystals in a mesh bag, secure the bag in the river, and immerse the crystals for a day or two.

- *Fire*: Light incense and pass crystals through the smoke. In a pinch, you can also wave them through the flame of a candle. The candle flame method is especially good for times when numerous people have touched your stones, like during a party or if you are working at a psychic fair. At many public gatherings, it is prohibited to light incense out of respect for allergenic sensitivities.

  [Note: crystal etiquette dictates that one should ask permission before feeling another person's crystals. This is because a particular stone may be in the process of being used for an intention exercise and needs to only involve the owner's energy.]

- *Earth*: Bury crystals for a week or two in the yard or in the soil of a potted plant.

- *Sun and Moonbeams*: For sunbeams, place crystals in direct sunlight anywhere from one day up to one week (depending on how fast they clear). Remove each day at dusk, and then replace in the morning. For moonbeams, it is best to place stones on a window ledge or table that will catch full rays. During the full moon is the most beneficial, as this phase produces the most light. Placing crystals in sun or moonbeams also recharges them with Universal Energies and can make their properties stronger.

# Crystal Uses for Home or Office

Crystals placed throughout your residence or workplace can greatly enhance the overall energy of these locations, causing you, your family, and guests to be more peaceful, creative, and balanced. Pets can also derive benefits from living in homes full of positive crystal energies!

To help increase your psychic awareness and integration with your outer self, create a simple altar that incorporates a few crystals. Designate a special spot in your favorite room and place symbols representing the four elements on a table, bookcase shelf, or window ledge. Such symbols may include a dish of water (water element), a candle (fire element), incense or a feather (air element), and, of course, crystals (earth element). Creatively add to this altar a beautiful cloth, flowers, a plant, a bell or chimes, or anything else that has spiritual significance for you. This altar is now ready to be used as a focal point for grounding and centering, to meditate in front of, and as the site for cleansing and programming your crystals.

Other good crystal locations for your home or office include under your bed—and the beds of your family members—to help produce restful sleep (see further discussion in Chapter 8), on top of an answering machine to guard against unwanted calls, and on top of the soil in indoor potted plants to make them grow more rapidly and with fewer diseases. It is usually best to have at least one crystal in every room, including the bathrooms. By doing so, you are balancing the general energy in your residence. As an added bonus, a crystal's beauty does wonders for all styles of interior decorating!

# 8

# *Working with Dreams &*
# *Guides*

True psychic development also involves calling upon those parts of ourselves that exist on other planes. When we access our intuition through subconscious dreaming and contact with our guides, we often deepen the types of messages we receive. In addition, knowing we have assistance from these two sources can provide great comfort as we continue to delve more intensely into our psychic core and seek to understand old blocks and difficult experiences.

## Dreamwork

As we develop our psychic self, it is common to have more dreams. This occurrence is due to the fact that our psychic side is linked to our subconscious, which activates our dream state. As we dig deeper into our intuitive center, it is also typical to more frequently remember our dreams. Dreams can be so wonderful: their rich imagery and symbolic messages assist us in understanding the complexity of our ongoing emotional and spiritual growth.

We can learn to request important messages from our dreams and can even direct them in order to receive clarification on prior information received. For dream direction, create an affirmative statement that states to your higher self, and the Universal Energies, what you wish to achieve. In designing an affirmative statement, always start with the "I" pronoun, and put it in the future tense by using the word "will." For instance, try repeating to yourself as you are getting into that drowsy state while lying in bed, "I will receive an important message in a dream tonight" or, even more to the point, "I will remember my dreams upon awakening in the morning." If you wish to go back into a prior dream to continue its story line or to figure out one of its components, repeat a very specific affirmation, such as, "I will go back into the house dream and find out what the cracked window in the bedroom means." This type of statement also helps in figuring out the gist of repeated dream themes.

Dream affirmations can take up to two weeks to take effect, so do not become discouraged if no dream messages come through right away. Have your journal, a pen, and a small flashlight by your bedside so it is easy for you to record any snippets upon awakening. Alternatively, some people find it easier to use a small tape recorder that they can speak into and transcribe later. With dreams, even recording your first feeling after waking up can be as important as listing actual details. Such emotions can give great insight into your psychic core and help you uncover blocks or long-standing attitudes about yourself and others.

In addition, we can set up our bedrooms in a way that will encourage more dreams of a deeply spiritual and educational nature. If it is possible, rearrange the direction of your bed so your head is facing north when you lay down. Facing north allows our energetic bodies to align with the magnetic energies of the Earth and can produce both a more restful sleep and a dream state in which we travel further into our psychic core. As an alternative, if it is not possible to move your bed, it is just as beneficial to place a medium-sized clear quartz crystal on the floor or rug underneath it, right below your head. I heard a wonderful success story about using crystals under beds from a former student who has infant twin girls. Her babies had severe bouts of colic, which would exacerbate during the night and cause them—and her—many sleepless nights. This mother placed a crystal beneath each crib and, within one week, her twins were sleeping through the night!

Keep track of your attempts to direct dreams and request information from your subconscious. With practice, you will learn what types of affirmations you best respond to, which will allow you to more rapidly receive needed and helpful information. Such knowledge can then be incorporated into your waking-state psychic work.

## Your Helpful Guides

All of us have guides, both in human and animal form, who are present around us at various times and for various reasons. Primarily, they exist to assist us on our spiritual paths and they make themselves known to us at precisely the right times. When are these right times? When we are going through a particularly rough period, when we feel very alone, when we need a direct message to help with a decision or transition, or when we are ready to turn a corner and begin our next life chapter. Sometimes guides emerge when we are born; other times they appear for a certain length of time to aid with a specific issue or series of events. It is important to recognize we have guides and that we are psychically evolving not just through our limited human experience. Our guides are parts of ourselves, but they exist on another level, a higher vibration, where the physical form is no longer needed.

You may have already met some of your guides through dreams, meditations, or visions. Once a guide has announced itself, we can always call upon this teacher in the future to ask further questions, get clarification on a prior message, or simply to request more unconditional love energy.

Below is a guided meditation that allows you to meet a human entity guide (animal spirit messengers will be discussed in the next chapter). Like the other scripted meditations in this book, you may first wish to record it by reading it aloud and then playing it back for yourself during a meditative session. Have your journal and pen handy so that afterward you can jot down which guide appeared and your initial experiences with this wonderful being.

### Meet a Guide—Read Very Slowly—Time: 8–10 Minutes

Sit or recline comfortably…close your eyes…and ground yourself by sending out tree roots from the soles of your feet and the base of your spine…have these tree roots go through the floor and anchor them deeply into Mother Earth…slow your breath down and take very deep breaths, filling your lungs and torso completely…**[pause for 1.5 minutes]**…continue to relax…and gently release any thoughts about what happened earlier in the day or yesterday…gently release any thoughts about what you need to do later or tomorrow…release tension from any part of your body by sending your breath there…**[pause for 15 seconds]**…continue to relax, slowing the breath down…focus on feeling how your breath circulates throughout your body…**[pause for 45 seconds]**…now place yourself in the center of an oval-shaped meadow…there's soft, cushy, green grass under your feet and all along the perimeter of the meadow are trees and low bushes…it's a beautiful, spring day and you can feel the sunlight on your skin and there's a warm breeze…no one else is around…this is a very special, sacred meadow…you're simply gazing around the meadow, taking in its shape and beautiful foliage…you feel very relaxed and peaceful…**[pause for 10 seconds]**…as you continue to gaze around the meadow, you think you see a slight movement out of the corner of your left eye…you're not quite sure you saw anything, so you turn slightly to face that direction…as you look in that direction, you see another small movement, a rustling in one of the low bushes…you're feeling very curious and continue to gaze in that direction…**[pause for 10 seconds]**…you see another rustling and then a person steps out from behind the low bush and stands fully upright…this person is facing you directly and is gazing at you from the edge of the meadow…you don't feel frightened at all…in fact, you sense that this entity is very friendly…you're simply gazing at each other...from where you are standing in the center of the meadow, just take this other person in...note its gender, style of dress, height, approximate age, and all other details...**[pause for 10 seconds]**...as you're standing peacefully, this person begins to walk toward you...you patiently wait for this person to approach...as this wonderful Being comes closer, you can make out a few more details...and now this beautiful entity is standing right in front of you and you gaze peacefully into its eyes...you can tell that here is a true friend and guide...you can feel the wisdom coming from this person...**[pause]**...as you're standing there, ask this guide a question: "Why are you here?"...and note if there's an answer...**[pause for 10 seconds]**...ask this guide a second question: "What is your name?"...and note if there's an answer...**[pause for 10 seconds]**...now ask your guide a third question: "What do I need to do right now?"...and note if there's an answer...**[pause for 10 seconds]**...now go ahead and begin to take a stroll with your guide around the meadow...you may want to hold hands or link arms...you're enjoying your interaction and it feels both extremely peaceful <u>and</u> rejuvenating...you feel so good that your guide has chosen to appear before you at this time...you remind yourself that you can meet your guide again whenever you need to...to ask more questions...to receive <u>more</u> unconditional love and nurturing...you continue to interact together in the meadow with your special guide...**[pause for 10 seconds]**...now come to a stop wherever you are in the meadow with your guide and give your guide a warm embrace, telling yourself that you can call upon your guide at any time for further work...the two of you part and your guide gently turns to walk back toward the perimeter of the meadow...you don't feel sad because you know you can meet your guide again whenever you feel the need...you watch your guide depart and feel very loved and nurtured, safe with the knowledge that you have assistance in this world...**[pause for 10 seconds]**...now take a super deep, cleansing breath...and take another super deep, cleansing breath…and take another super deep, cleansing breath and stretch your arms up and over your head…and you can open your eyes when you feel ready.

*Henry, 49, was a mortgage broker for a multi-branch real estate firm. For the most part, he enjoyed his work, but over the last few years had started to feel rather stagnant. He was beginning to view the public he interacted with as a nuisance instead of people he could potentially assist. He certainly did not like these feelings. As a result of recent discussions with his wife, who enjoyed her profession as a social worker, he was starting to entertain the idea of switching careers. After all, they no longer had major debt and had no children, so the timing seemed good for Henry to focus on uncovering his life purpose. He felt excited at the prospect, but also experienced quite a bit of trepidation. What if he could not decide on another career direction? If he did attempt a new course, what if he failed?*

*During class, I reminded Henry of the importance to relax into the transitional process and not to put any pressure on himself. He already was used to going quite deep in his meditations, and I felt the Meet a Guide exercise would be particularly effective at this point in his life. Here are the journal pages he turned in describing his experience:*

*"After dinner, I went into my home office and laid down on the small couch I have in there. I felt very relaxed and, after grounding myself with my tree roots, began my deep, loop breathing. I took my time and gave myself a few extra minutes to concentrate on my breath as it circulated throughout my body.*

*"I had already recorded the Meet a Guide script and began to play it. In my mind's eye, I conjured up the oval-shaped meadow and placed myself right in the middle of it. The meadow felt quite nurturing with its soft grass and warm sunlight. I enjoyed taking in all of its surrounding foliage, and even heard a few songbirds in the background.*

*"Just as prompted, I did see the rustling in the low bush and waited for my higher self to present this guide to me. And who appeared? A beautiful young woman stepped out from behind the bush. She was probably about twenty or twenty-two and looked of Nordic descent, with her tall, slender*

body and straight, light blonde hair. Since she wore a metal breastplate, a helmet of some sort that covered her forehead, and sturdy boots, I decided she must be some kind of warrior. In one of her hands she carried a long spear. Her face looked very determined and intense as she focused on me. However, I felt no fear when she began to walk toward me.

"When she got within a few feet, she stopped directly in front of me. I could feel a very calm energy emanating from my guide. When I asked her the first question, 'Why are you here?,' she answered, 'I'm here to help you uncover your true gifts.' When I asked her the second question, 'What is your name?,' she gave a name I had never heard before. The best way I can write it phonetically is Tsah-kléen-drah. I took this name to be part of an ancient language from an old civilization. Tsah-kléen-drah's answer to my third question, 'What do I need to do right now?' was 'You need to ethically help others.' This last answer puzzled me—I've always been a highly ethical person. I knew I would reflect upon her statement in the coming week.

"We began to walk around the meadow. Then, suddenly, my guide took my hand and I was instantly transported with her to another scene. It felt like my body zoomed upward and we flew through the heavens. We landed at the outskirts of some sort of modern-day city plaza with a lot of people gathered together. They were all looking at a stage and podium set up at one end. On the stage was a middle-aged man giving a speech, and I was standing there with him, slightly to the side and a little behind. I wasn't talking and I believe I was his advisor or manager. I knew I was observing this scene from afar with Tsah-kléen-drah, but I also felt my presence up on stage in this new role. And it felt good.

"Tsah-kléen-drah took my hand again and again we flew upward, landing back in the meadow. We strolled a bit more, and then I could feel it was time for her to go. When we embraced, I could sense the spiritual force within her and feel her unconditional love for me. I silently thanked her for coming."

Henry reported during our next class session that he thought a great deal about this first meeting with his wonderful guide. He said the scene in the city plaza gave him courage to pursue an idea he had long held of becoming *an assistant to a politician, or other public figure, who was focused on making people's lives better. Because he already had many years of experience in the housing industry, Henry could see himself on a committee for developing affordable housing or bringing a new homeless shelter into existence. Perhaps, he told us, he could make contacts in such a committee that would lead to a managerial role. He wanted to somehow impact people in a more direct manner—especially those who did not have the skills or knowledge to do it themselves. His initial experience with his Nordic warrior guide gave him the needed impetus to look into this new career path. Henry knew that subsequent meetings with Tsah-kléen-drah would produce more helpful and insightful information.*

I encourage you to contact your guide many times, ask many questions, and get to know him or her well. You may find it particularly helpful to ask the third question, "What do I need to do right now?" at the close of each visit with your guide. The answers received to this query will allow you to stay dynamic in your approach to your psychic development. In time, this guided meditation will also produce additional guides. As with your first teacher, deeply bonding with these other helpers will let you obtain relevant and highly spiritual messages. The more comfortable you become with your guides, the more information you are likely to receive.

# 9

## *Animal Spirit Messengers*

Besides human entity guides who come into our lives to assist us on our spiritual paths and aid in our psychic development, wonderful animal spirits also exist as divine helpers. These special creatures come in all varieties of species and, like their human counterparts, remain available to us for varying lengths of time. Recognizing and working with animal envoys can be a very powerful and no-nonsense experience as this type of guide utilizes physical postures, as well as more conventional methods of communicating, to reveal important, intuitive-based messages. Because animals usually act in a visceral manner, they are automatically at an advanced stage of spiritual development; after all, psychic development directly incorporates listening to one's gut instinct.

## Historical Animal Reverence

In many ancient societies, animal archetypes were deified to assist the leaders, and general populace, in imparting important societal values and achieving necessary seasonal goals. For instance, Egypt of long ago revered the cat goddess Bastet (also known as Bast). Bastet was honored as a symbol of fertility—both for the community crops and for procreation—and also was considered a protector of the dead. In fact, many flesh-and-blood cats were mummified and buried along with their owners. The ancient Egyptians thought so highly of cats that at one point in this society's history, cat gods outnumbered human gods.

For most Native American tribes, animal spirits were, and still are, often consulted. Many native peoples consider all creatures as teachers and believe these guides have habit patterns that relay useful information to humans. To give an example, the tenacity of a spider in building its web can send an important message to someone who tends to procrastinate or give up too quickly when trying to complete a project. On a more spiritual level, elders of some of these societal groups used animal parts, like teeth or bits of hair, for divination purposes. Such items were either picked or spilled out of a pouch and then interpreted according to the pattern they displayed.

## Teachers or Protectors

Animal spirit messengers primarily fall into one of two categories: that of a teacher or that of a protector. Teacher guides assist with life lessons—both major and minor—and help us to successfully cope with day-to-day stresses. Protector animals help lessen negative thoughts and energies, both self-produced ones and those encountered in the outside world. Protector spirits also make sure we don't veer too far from our spiritual paths. Of course, animal guides do exist that are a mixture of these two groups, but each animal, nonetheless, will demonstrate more beneficial energy in one of the roles.

How can we tell if an animal guide is more of a teacher or more of a protector? By its body posture when you first see him or her in a dream, meditation, or vision. For instance, if the animal is touching you (e.g., a bird sitting on your shoulder), or actually wrapped around you (e.g., a snake looped around your leg), this wonderful spirit would be a protector. If the animal is beckoning you to follow, or nudging you with its nose or body, that guide would be a teacher. Teacher animals are also known for giving extremely direct verbal messages too!

# Significance of Animal Species

Animal messengers encompass five very different classes of creatures. All types impart specific lessons that serve to show us how to both enhance and further our psychic growth. To help you understand why particular guides appear, review the descriptions below of what each species represents. Recognizing these overall qualities will allow you to better absorb, and then put into practice, the personal messages received from your individual guides.

**Winged animals:** because these spirits fly, they want us to soar and reach for our goals. The act of flying is, in and of itself, a symbol of freedom, since one leaves the gravitational pull of the Earth to connect with the sky. When a winged creature, such as a bird, appears as a guide, it sends an overall message not to curtail your own freedom. In addition, because many flying animals sail toward a destination in a very focused manner (e.g., an annual migratory route), a secondary message may involve encouragement to stay on course toward a goal.

**Earthbound mammals:** depending on their size, these warm-blooded guides convey important lessons, while remaining empathetic and nurturing. Large animals, like horses, lions, and bears, symbolize strength, perseverance, and groundedness. Small spirits, like rabbits, squirrels, and foxes, represent intelligence, quiet accomplishments, and working through fears. Earthbound mammal messengers often remain with us for many years at a time and can sometimes be traced back to initially appearing during one's early childhood.

**Fish and other waterborne creatures:** these lovely, swimming guides help uncover our innermost intuitive layers. First of all, because such spirits live in water, they assist us to be more fluid and flexible, just like their environment. In addition, especially if a fish has appeared, it could be sending a message dealing with teamwork, since fish often swim in schools. Lastly, the element of water is a common symbol for the subconscious and so waterborne guides can aid us in digging more deeply into our psyche and psychicness.

**Reptiles:** these prehistoric beings primarily stand for regeneration and rebirth, since many (like snakes) periodically shed their skin, while others (like lizards) can regrow appendages. Also, because reptiles are cold-blooded, they need to bask for long periods in the sun. By doing so, they are showing us the importance of taking time to be still, go within, and replenish our energy. What better way to become more comfortable in asking ourselves for spiritual and growth-oriented messages!

**Insects:** despite their size, these minute guides represent lofty and substantive life-enriching lessons. Since they do not have a brain, but instead possess synapses imprinted with drives, insects can help prevent us from veering away from goals. This type of spirit messenger also sends reminders to stay focused and industrious (think of a caterpillar weaving a delicate cocoon), to utilize one's ingenuity (think of an ant lifting an object many times its body weight), and to work as a team (think of a cockroach colony invading a kitchen). Most importantly perhaps, is an insect guide's profound message to make the most of one's life. Because insects have a very short life span, they want us to fully develop our psychic side, without becoming too distracted or fatigued from using our energy for inconsequential things.

## Working with Your Animal Spirit Messengers

As with human entity spirit guides, it is extremely beneficial to have an ongoing relationship with your animal guides. The more you work with your wonderful creatures, the more assistance you will receive, and you will find yourself feeling more psychically integrated and intuitive. When an animal being first appears in a dream, meditation, or vision, go over the following checklist to initially learn as much as possible about your new, otherworldly friend. Jotting down your responses to these points will help you in subsequent consultations.

### Animal Spirit Messenger Checklist

- Determine your guide's main purpose: that of teacher or that of protector. What is the animal's initial posture in relation to yourself? Touching you, or nudging/leading?

- Study your guide's appearance: what type of coloring does it have? What do these colors mean to you? Keep in mind that you may see colors on your animal that differ from what you would see in nature. Pay particular attention to your spirit guide's eye color, the proverbial "window to the soul." The animal's eye color can be a reflection of what is to be uncovered in your own soul.

- Try to figure out your guide's gender and age: is your creature male or female? Is it young, middle-aged, or elderly? What traits do you associate with these gender and age groups?

- Listen and look for any messages: is your animal spirit communicating in some way? This could be verbally (even in a foreign language), telepathically, or through body language.

- Ask your animal guide questions: "Why are you here?" "How long have you been with me?" "What is your name?" It also helps to periodically ask, "What do I need to do right now?"

In addition to the above, you may wish to draw a rough sketch of your guide or cut out a picture of that species. By tacking up a visual representation of your spirit animal (for instance, onto a mirror or refrigerator), you will more quickly bond with him or her. You will also have a wonderful, continual reminder of a loving being dedicated to your psychic development.

*Brenda, 37, was a veterinarian who had always known about the spiritual side of animals. Ever since she could remember, she had experienced visits from her creature friends in dreams and visions whenever she was going through a hard time. Her earliest memory took place when she was about one year old, when a fluffy, white rabbit materialized in her crib, and gently rocked her when she was afraid of the dark.*

*Brenda knew she would become a vet and, early in her training, decided to focus on large animals, including zoo residents. Because of her knack for rapidly putting her patients at ease and gaining their trust, she was often consulted to help with particularly difficult cases.*

*In our class, Brenda expressed interest in deepening her bond with one of her long-term guides, a huge, black, grizzly bear. However, much to her amazement, a new animal spirit came to greet her during our guided meditation. I told Brenda afterward that it is quite common to expect (or even wish for) a particular animal messenger before this exercise begins and then be pleasantly surprised by who actually appears.*

*Similar to the Meet a Guide meditation in the previous chapter, I took Brenda and her classmates to a beautiful meadow lined with trees and bushes. Here is what transpired for this deeply spiritual vet:*

*"When I turned to look toward the direction of the rustling leaves, a giraffe unfolded its long neck and legs, stood at its full height, and stepped out from behind a clump of bushes and trees. I was so surprised to see this creature instead of my bear! Of course, I was thrilled and felt quite excited as this beautiful, African animal started to slowly and gracefully walk toward me.*

*"Just as you taught us, I remembered to take in all of the giraffe's details. I felt right away that it was female and noted that she seemed taller than most females you'd find in the wild. I was also drawn to her large, dark brown eyes. They showed extreme compassion and wisdom and their deep color reminded me of rich earth. I also loved her soft golden color and tan spots. These colors were very soothing. She felt quite young, maybe three or four years old at most.*

*"When my giraffe guide stopped in front of me, she laid her head across my right shoulder. I took this to symbolize that she primarily is a protector spirit and has appeared to assist me with taking care of business in the outside world. In my field, there is still some divisiveness between two schools of thought on animal care. I don't believe in dominating an animal and forc-*

*ing treatment. I try to enlighten, in a gentle way, of course, my colleagues who are more old school. This greeting posture of the giraffe's felt utterly nurturing and safe. I didn't want her 'hug' to end!*

*"After she finished this welcome embrace and again stood at her full height, I began to ask her those suggested questions. The answers I received all came telepathically. To the first one, 'Why are you here?' I got the response, 'To help you reach new heights in your career.' Well, it wasn't hard for me to figure out the connection between such a tall animal and my wish for advancement in my work. I'm at a point where I'm trying to gain more recognition with my international colleagues so that I can collaborate with them on their tough cases.*

*"To the second question, 'What is your name?' I did not receive an answer and took this to mean that I would be told in the near future. To the third question, 'How long have you been with me?' my giraffe said she started assisting me two years ago. I tried to remember what occurred around that time and knew she was referring to my presentation of a scientific paper at a veterinary conference. This report described my rather unorthodox, but more humane, method for bonding with new patients. My lecture turned out to be a highlight of the seminar and was written up in the local newspaper.*

*"To the last question, 'What do I need to do right now?' she told me to finish a second paper I had started and submit it to my favorite scientific journal. I had been debating whether to complete this piece, as I wasn't sure it would appeal to a wide enough audience. Well, now I had the extra encouragement I needed!*

*"I really enjoyed meeting my new giraffe guide and plan on contacting her again later this week. Not only do I want to find out her name, but also I'm eager to discover how I can work with her and learn to be a more effective doctor. It's important to me to continue to make a difference with the animals."*

# 10

# *Past-Lives & Reincarnation: Windows to Your Energetic Past*

I used to be a big skeptic when it came to the idea of reincarnation. I could not understand why some people had extremely difficult or crime-filled lives and, according to karmic and past-life theories, would choose these lifestyles full of suffering. But then, in 1986, I had a very powerful dream about myself in medieval France that seemed to mirror a heavy emotional situation I was experiencing at the time. I did not equate that this dream was, in actuality, a past-life remembrance until one year later, when I asked a psychic reader to tap into one of my past lives. Well, the young man recited my dream verbatim!

Since this occurrence, I have been studying various schools of thought about reincarnation, particularly the need for the soul to return numerous times in human form in order to complete important lessons, to interact with certain individuals, and to finish psychic evolvement. In addition, many past-life proponents believe we choose our parents each time around. Reflecting on how you and your family interacted during your formative years can help you understand part of your mission for this lifetime. For instance, if you and your parents and siblings were often at odds, a portion of your life purpose could involve exploring how to forgive. If you were adopted, this could indicate the need to experience lessons concerned with abandonment, perseverance, independence, and belonging.

You may have already gotten inklings into your past lives. Good initial indicators include being drawn to a particular country or culture, ease in learning a foreign language, and instantly "recognizing" and feeling comfortable with a stranger whom you have just met. When you learn various techniques to help you flesh out these inklings and get a more comprehensive picture of a particular past life, you can then figure out similarities to your current lifetime and understand why you are directing it in a certain manner. We do direct most aspects of our lives, because in every situation we have choices. We may not always be aware of all choices available to us, but they are there nonetheless and become revealed when we are ready or in a particular stage of our psychic development.

Calling up past-life details primarily occurs through dreams and meditation. Below are the techniques involved with both modalities.

## Past-Life Memories through Dreams

As discussed in Chapter 8, we can give ourselves dream auto-suggestions that ask our higher selves to send us specific types of information. To access past-life dream messages, try the following affirmations while you are lying in bed, getting into that very relaxed, drowsy state: "I will receive a dream containing a past-life memory tonight," or "I will free up imagery of a past-life experience in a dream this evening." You may not immediately dream the first night after reciting your affirmation, but repeat this exercise for a number of consecutive nights and you will likely achieve success.

Be sure to jot down any snippets of imagery, story lines, or characters contained in past-life information received from your dream state. These snippets can be expanded upon in subsequent dreams merely by asking for more details. You may also find it helpful to record the exact affirmation used; that way, you can structure other requests in a similar manner. Finally, think about parallels you can draw between past-life dream messages and events in your current life. Can you recognize any similarities or repetition of experiences?

## Past-Life Memories through Meditation

To access past-life information during a meditative session, light a candle, and set it near you on a table or on the floor. Ground yourself and begin loop breathing. When you feel centered and cleared of the stimuli from the day, begin to repeat (either aloud or silently) the following three sentences: "Who am I?" "Who was I?" "Who will I be?" Say these phrases slowly and in the same order at least five to seven times. They will help you get into a semi-trance state and will let you become relaxed enough for your psychic self to send you messages and imagery. Just allow whatever bubbles up to come through and do not put pressure on yourself. If you do not receive information during this first attempt, take a break, and then repeat the three sentences a few more times (or try another day). Again, even if only snippets of information surface, you can always ask for expansion during a subsequent session. As with receiving past-life messages through dreams, keep track of all information revealed, and try to recognize the origins of certain present-day behavior, or choices, based on your new past-life revelations.

*Isaac, 73, was the oldest student I had ever had in a class. A life-long free thinker, over the years he had taken part in numerous demonstrations that encompassed all sorts of issues: politics, union disputes, destruction of the environment, etc. He also enjoyed reading about different spiritual philosophies and had attended many lectures and retreats featuring well-known authors. Of late, he was particularly interested in remembering his past lives—and became even more so after we discussed in class how our past lives often provide pertinent information about fears and preferences we carry into our current life. Isaac wanted to uncover the origins of a couple of his overriding personality traits.*

*He volunteered to perform the Past-Life Meditation before the entire class. First, I asked Isaac to bring his chair to the front of the room. I then lit a white candle and placed it on a small table beside him. After he grounded himself and began his loop breathing, he closed his eyes and began to slowly repeat the three, short phrases that would take him to a deeper, past-life level: "Who Am I?" "Who Was I?" "Who Will I Be?" I reminded Isaac to relax and to repeat these sentences as many times as he needed. The following is an account of what transpired that evening for this fascinating, elderly gentleman:*

*"I feel a sharp, cold wind on my face and can smell salty, sea water. I can't tell where I am yet, but I think I'm on a large boat…yes, now I can feel a rocking motion and a sense of forward movement. There are a few crewmembers on the boat with me, but they're more in the background. I'm getting a sense that I'm the one in charge; I'm the captain."*

*I gently interjected and asked Isaac what he looked like as this ship's captain and if he could get a sense of his personality or emotional state. Keeping his eyes closed, he picked up where he left off:*

*"When I first saw myself in this lifetime, I saw a tall, rather heavyset man with a full, red beard. I believe I was a very determined person and very capable as a sailor and leader. But I also sense an underlying loneliness. Since I didn't see myself interacting with the crew, I wonder if I spent a lot of time alone on the long voyages I took. Perhaps I had a wife and children and missed them terribly?"*

*I again quietly prompted Isaac and asked him if he had difficulty in his current lifetime being alone or had ever felt cutoff from loved ones.*

*"Early in my sales career, I had to go on several short business trips. I remember feeling extremely anxious when apart from my wife, Gloria, and I remember her reassuring me over and over that everything would be OK. I never could understand why being away for only a few days would make me so stressed out. I used to rationalize my anxiety by blaming it on nerves over meeting new contacts on these trips."*

*In order to go a bit deeper into his past-life memory, I told Isaac to close his eyes again and take a few more deep breaths. I wanted to see if any other information would bubble through for him. He did so and continued:*

*"I also see on the ship many large, round, wooden containers with lids. I see myself walking over to these containers and lifting a few of the lids to*

*check on their contents. Inside the barrels are brightly colored powders. Because I'm now beginning to smell wonderful odors, I think these must be spices! If these are spices, then I must have been a captain who traveled to the Orient or to India to import spices. Did these long trade routes from Europe to other continents occur in the sixteenth and seventeenth centuries? I'll have to double check in a history book tomorrow."*

*"Isaac," I asked, "what parallel do spices and pleasing odors hold for you now?"*

*"Well, I started getting into cooking and making up recipes about five years ago. My wife and friends say I am a natural and that I missed my calling, so to speak, by not being a professional chef. But I figure that if I can enjoy this talent now and create wonderful dishes, it doesn't really matter that I've discovered this skill at my age. I've never felt that anything is ever a mistake or that one can 'miss a calling.'"*

*Many of Isaac's classmates voiced their agreement with this last statement. I was pleased that he had received such rich imagery. The class and I talked a bit more about the relevance our past lives have with our current lifetime and I could tell, when our session ended, that the other students were eager to return home and try their own Past-Life Meditation.*

Whichever method for revealing past-life information works best for you, periodically perform that technique. You may also wish to alternate between designing dream affirmations and performing the three-phrase meditation. Since most people have been reincarnated many times, it helps to know about as many former lives as possible. Such information can then allow us to better understand how we can integrate and use our past-life experiences in the lifetime we chose this time around.

# 11

## *Gauge Your Psychic Progress with Psychometry*

Psychometry is a wonderfully informative divination method that requires you to access two of your five psychic senses: clairsentience (touch) and clairvoyance (sight). At this point in time, you are ready to learn and practice this technique. After all, you have been working hard on revealing more of your intuitive self and recognizing how your psychic side sends you messages. As a beginner, psychometry is an excellent tool to add to your repertoire, and by completing the following exercise, you will be able to see how far you truly have come with your psychic development. Psychometry produces interesting intuitive information and, in the process, strengthens your ability to trust your inner voice.

## What is Psychometry?

In psychometry, we receive psychic impressions from an inanimate object, like a piece of jewelry, a photograph, or an article of clothing. The type of information acquired can be about the object's current owner, any prior owners, the creator of the object, or how the object is—or was—used. Oftentimes, psychometry produces messages about emotional states a former or present owner is undergoing and can be quite helpful in understanding how best to interact with that person. Following the steps below, give this technique a try with a family heirloom or with something belonging to an acquaintance. Then solicit feedback to assess your accuracy. Remember to first ask permission to read this item if it is not yours.

### The Art of Psychometry

- Gaze at the object, either in your hands, or lay it on a table in front of you. Look at the item from all angles.

- Record in your journal any initial snippets received (words, feelings, colors).

- Hold the object in your left hand (remember our left side is receptive and deals more with the metaphysical). Note any warmth, coolness, etc. *Give yourself a few minutes.*

- Next, close your eyes and place the item over your third eye. Note and record any snippets of information. *Give yourself a few minutes.*

- Next, keeping your eyes closed, place the object over your heart. Note and record any snippets of information. *Give yourself a few minutes.*

- Open your eyes and again gaze at the item, checking for any other pieces of information.

- Report your findings to the owner (or to someone who knew the owner) and ask for feedback.

As with all metaphysical modalities, do not pressure yourself for 100 percent accuracy and do not think that any snippet of information received is not worth recording and reporting. Sometimes the most insignificant-feeling image, word, or color can, in actuality, be the crux of that object's meaning to its owner.

*Renée, 32, was a wonderfully intuitive young woman whom I was mentoring to be a psychic reader. We had been working for a while with various metaphysical tools and she had a good grasp of how these modalities both confirmed and enhanced her own innate abilities. I next wanted her to gain experience with psychometry. Actually, she was somewhat familiar with this technique, since she had been on the receiving end during a read-ing from me a couple of years ago. For that appointment, she brought an inherited, antique brooch from a distant great aunt's estate and I was able to describe, among other things, the deceased woman's physical appearance and fondness for horses.*

*Renée came to my house full of energy and ready to learn. She was so much fun to teach and I already could envision her animatedly talking to clients as she read them. We sat at my kitchen table and I reviewed with her how to prepare for performing psychometry. I told her she would need to get into a very deep, quiet space within herself and ask her inner voice to be receptive to any and all messages. I also went over the various ways to read an inanimate object: gazing directly at it, holding it in the left hand, over the third eye with eyes closed, and/or against the heart chakra. For our practice session, I would record Renée's impressions; that way, she would not have to pause in her flow to jot down information she received.*

*I then excused myself to get the piece of jewelry I had earlier selected for Renée. When I brought it back to the table, she let out a big, "Wow!" I was not surprised. What I placed before her was a beautiful, ornate, opal brace-let. The iridescent, oval-shaped stones were set end-to-end between lovely filigree 18K links. The design of the bracelet evoked a Victorian feeling.*

*"OK, Renée, close your eyes, ground yourself, and begin your deep breathing," I instructed. "When you feel centered and relaxed, open your eyes and gaze at the bracelet."*

*I watched as she took her time and journeyed to the receptive space within herself, where she could hear her inner voice. Renée then opened her eyes, picked up the piece of jewelry, and looked at it from all angles.*

*"This bracelet feels very substantial in my hands and I'll bet it was owned by someone who liked to stand out in a crowd," she began. "I also can feel it start to warm as I'm holding it—is that because the stones are heating up?"*

*I didn't reply, but with my eyes encouraged Renée to continue. At this point, my sole task was to write down all she said.*

*"Even though I'm feeling some warmth from the bracelet, parts of it still feel cool. Could this person have blown hot and cold or had a very frosty side at times?"*

Renée paused for a moment to close her eyes and take a few deep breaths. She next held the bracelet over her third eye. I could see how centered she was becoming as she focused on the jewelry piece. I gently prompted her by asking if she could get a visual image of the owner.

*"I'm seeing a tall, young woman with dark hair swept up into a bun on the top of her head. She feels full of energy and rather impatient, like she'd lose her temper fast if you crossed her. She's wearing a long, cream-colored dress with ornate embroidery on it, so I take that to mean she was well off."*

Renée now moved the bracelet to hold it over her heart. Her eyes remained closed and I asked her to focus on the emotional state of the object's former owner.

*"I get a real restlessness from this woman. I wonder if she was held back from pursuing her dreams or a particular goal?"* Renée paused for a second and I saw her brow wrinkle in concentration. *"I just got a quick flash of her showing the bracelet to a shop owner!"* she blurted out. *"She was leaning over a glass counter and a man was looking at it in an appraising way. I guess she may have tried to sell the bracelet."*

I was furiously taking notes and, as soon as I jotted down Renée's last statement, I asked her to again hold the bracelet in both hands and gaze at it a few more minutes. She took several deep breaths and opened her eyes.

*"I'm not really getting anything else,"* she said, after a short time. *"But I do feel this woman loved this bracelet and that it held great meaning for her. To me, the stones still feel infused with her dynamic spirit."*

I thanked Renée for doing such a great job of obtaining so many details about the bracelet and its previous owner. Before giving her feedback, I looked over my notes so I could confirm, as much as possible, the different snippets of information she had received.

*"This opal bracelet belonged to my maternal great-grandmother Agnes. From what my grandmother told my mother and me, Agnes was a woman before her time. She was very independent and longed to do her own thing.*

*But because she lived in a time when women were not recognized for their business sense and sense of adventure, she carried around a lot of anger and frustration. The opal bracelet was a wedding gift from her rather domineering husband, and Agnes did, at one point, have it appraised. She seriously considered escaping her somewhat stifling lifestyle and knew the sale of her beautiful jewelry piece could help fund her plans.*

*"My mother said Agnes never followed through because she was afraid of being ostracized in whatever new town she chose. She did, however, become a music teacher who only accepted female students. My grandmother told me a few years ago that Agnes specifically decided to instruct girls because she wanted to teach them how to cultivate their business sense and how to effectively communicate with people. By only having girls in her classes, Agnes could safely discuss with them the importance of maintaining one's autonomy. I'm sure my great-grandmother felt she was contributing to the healthy development of her pupils and was helping them to be more balanced and satisfied as they became adults. Agnes definitely was a proponent of self-growth and figured out a way to assist young women, even while living in a pretty repressed society."*

*Renée was smiling broadly as I wrapped up my synopsis of great-grandmother Agnes, and I knew she was pleased with herself.*

*"I'm amazed at how much I picked up on just by holding Agnes' bracelet," she said. "You confirmed a lot of what I was seeing and feeling. Was my physical description of her accurate?"*

*"Yes, it was," I replied. "I have seen a picture of Agnes, and she did have long, dark hair and was tall. The one photo I have of her shows her in a very fancy dress and I do know that my mother's family moved to the U.S. with quite a bit of money. In addition, Agnes married into a well-to-do family. You did really well, Renée."*

*Renée and I talked a bit more about the psychometry session. I told her that when one rotates between gazing at the object, holding it over the third eye, and then against the heart, usually more information will come through. When we were all finished, I thanked her for coming over to prac-*

*tice, and sent her off with the notes I had taken so she would have a record of her first psychometry reading.*

What item did you use when trying this exercise? If you held and looked at a piece of jewelry, next time consider using a photograph. If you received information from an article of clothing, during your next attempt ask a family member for an old coin or small, decorative art piece. Many psychometry practitioners obtain the most details from a particular category of object. Similarly, you may find yourself doing the same. By knowing what items tend to produce a large amount of psychic information, you can then request such objects from friends, relatives, or future clients.

# 12

## *Importance of Ceremonies & Rituals*

As you become more deeply involved in your psychic development, you may feel inclined to create symbolic ceremonies. Human beings love rituals that honor their spirituality and values. Take the wedding ceremony, for instance. Two individuals come together to show a higher power (e.g., God), their friends, family, and society that they are choosing to connect their lives. Weddings are replete with ritual: walking down the aisle, throwing the bouquet, reciting vows. Rituals and ceremonies serve to make intentions and goals more concrete and infuse these objectives with a wonderful spiritual component.

Since receiving psychic information involves many symbols, incorporating symbols into a ritual can hold not only great meaning, but also can cause the ceremony itself to serve as a catalyst for further opening of your intuitive side. There are many books that contain rituals for specific purposes; these manuals can help you become familiar with myriad subjects that benefit from ritualization. However, I encourage you to design your own ceremonies that focus on releasing intentions through speaking and writing.

### Spoken-Word Rituals and Ceremonies

This type of ritual involves the use of props and invocations. People in all ancient societies participated in such ceremonies and they are just as effective today. Often, people like to perform Spoken-Word Ceremonies during different phases of the moon. In general, the moon represents spirituality, feminine intuition, and powerful, positive atmospheric energy. The following three moon phases are most appropriate for rituals. Their corresponding energetic definitions include:

New Moon (Waxing Moon): performed after the first sliver of a crescent appears. A time for new beginnings and enhanced creativity.

Full Moon: performed on the eve of the Full Moon. A time of fullness and change.

Dark Moon: performed on the Waning Moon. A time when there is an ending before new life starts. A time to discover, and uncover, your secrets and mysteries.

Presented below is a step-by-step guide to help you design a meaningful and growth-oriented event.

### Creating a Spoken-Word Ritual

- Decide what the ritual will honor or mark. Reaching a goal? Creating an open channel for receiving psychic information on a particular topic? Purging part of your past (specifically which part)?

- If multiple people participate in the ritual, stand with them in a circle. This geometric shape symbolizes continuity, movement, and intimacy. If you do the ceremony alone, stand facing north, which is the most effective direction for harnessing creativity.

- On a table or on the ground, place in front of you symbols representing the four natural elements (remember your home altar?). You need objects for earth, air, fire, and water. You may also wish to have a bell, or chimes, to strike during emphasis points in the ceremony (examples: at the opening, closing, or after certain words are spoken).

- Ground yourself and begin deep, loop breathing. Focus only on your breath and the ritual you are about to perform.

- Verbally invite into your ceremony all friendly entities of the Universe. This can include God, the Goddess, your higher self, and any and all guides.

- Make statements aloud about the ritual's purpose. You can also write on small slips of paper what your intentions are for the ceremony; e.g., what you are trying to release, bring toward you, etc. These slips of paper can then be tightly folded and burned, one by one, in a small receptacle. By burning written statements, you are assuring the release of your intentions into the Universe. After the ceremony, scatter or bury the ashes outside; never toss them into the garbage or flush down a toilet—discarding ashes in this manner keeps their energy in your home.

- Next, do a silent meditation and reflect on what has just been said and done. Visualize the outcome you want.

- When your meditation is finished, announce that the ceremony is over, and thank all invited entities for joining you and assisting with their energy.

*I invited four former students over one evening to take part in a New Moon ritual. Wanting a good balance for the group's energy, I phoned two women and two men: Katherine, 58, Patrick, 33, Tom, 41, and Julie, 29. All of them were pushing through important personal blocks that hampered their levels of success and I knew they needed help releasing old thought patterns. By doing so, they would free up more energy for their upcoming projects and be able to achieve further spiritual development.*

*After everyone arrived and exchanged pleasantries, we went into the living room to sit down and discuss our objective for the Spoken-Word Ritual. We decided to focus on shedding two deep-rooted, self-negating thoughts each—ones that made us automatically doubt ourselves. We also agreed to write what we wanted to purge on small slips of paper, which would be burned during the ritual. I had already prepared some narrow, blank pieces of lavender paper for our use.*

*I then brought the group into my spare room that I use for ceremonies. This room contains a coffee table in the middle, various sizes of green plants, and a couple of small tables against two of its walls. On the small tables I had placed pretty cloths in shades of blue and purple and softly burning yellow candles. The yellow candles signified our third chakras—the chakra that deals with taking risks and starting new ventures.*

*The coffee table was adorned with a large piece of beige lace and held four items to represent the four natural elements: a small decorative bowl of water (water element), a wild turkey feather (air element), multiple crystals (earth element), and a lit white candle (fire element). Katherine added a wonderful chime for us to ring and Patrick placed, at one end of the table, a bouquet of cut flowers from his garden. He said the flowers represented growth for everyone present. To complete the symbolic objects necessary for our ritual, I added the lavender slips of paper, pens, and a brass receptacle for burning our purge statements. All of us also held, or were wearing, personal power crystals or other significant articles.*

*We all stood in a circle around the coffee table, with myself at the north end, and grounded ourselves before beginning loop breathing. I asked the group to clear their minds and focus on the purpose of the ritual. Before reciting the invocation, I walked three times in a clockwise direction behind the participants, in order to delineate the circle. I then began:*

*"We welcome all friendly entities and guides into our circle for help with our ritual this evening on this New Moon. We welcome all guides who reside in the north, the magnetic center of the Universe and caretaker of all creative work. We welcome all guides who reside in the east, center of all life and all beginnings. We welcome all guides who reside in the south, center for the life-giving energy of the Sun. And we welcome all guides who reside in the west, center for renewing our intentions and recharging our energy and soul."*

*Before I continued, I slowly rang Katherine's chime three times to signify our desire to manifest and prepare for the future.*

*"We are gathered here this evening to utilize the New Moon energy to help us plant new ideas and start new projects that will enhance ourselves and those around us. In order to clear the path for these new projects, we need to release old thoughts that no longer serve us. That way, our higher selves and the Universal Energies will know we are truly ready. We will now do a short meditation to ask our inner voices for the two themes of neg-*

*ative thinking we need to purge. Once we decide, we will write down each release request on a separate piece of paper, tightly fold each slip, and then, one-by-one, light them with the candle flame."*

For a few moments, we paused with our eyes closed to silently reflect on what needed to be purged. The room's temperature soon increased with the increase of our individual core energy and a very focused atmosphere was felt by all. We then began to fill out our slips of lavender paper, being careful to fold each one accordion style. After all ten pieces of paper were completed, we took turns lighting them and then held the slips for as long as possible before dropping them into the brass bowl. It was fascinating to observe the different ways the folded paper incinerated. Some burned very fast, while others seemed hesitant to become engulfed. I was curious about the students' choices on what to purge and if their release statements corresponded to the burn patterns, but their decisions were private and needed to remain confidential. I felt extremely centered, focused, and cleansed and was sure the group felt similarly.

I next asked these wonderful people to do a second, short meditation that carried a dual purpose: to reflect upon what we had just asked to be eliminated and to direct our intentions about any upcoming projects out into the Universe. I told them to visualize themselves actually completing these projects, while feeling very positive and optimistic in the process.

After a few minutes, I ended the Spoken-Word Ritual: "Our New Moon ceremony is now over. We thank all of our guides and the Universal Energies for joining us and assisting us this evening as part of our ongoing growth and spiritual development. We are grateful for any and all guidance and look forward to future rituals."

I next gave each of the participants a chance to verbalize any feelings and observations produced by the ceremony. Afterward, I opened the circle by walking behind them all—but this time in a counter-clockwise direction. Finally, I poured the ashes from the brass receptacle into a small plastic bag that I would later scatter outside.

We retired to the living room to relax a bit and share more of how we felt during the Spoken-Word Ritual. Tom and Julie described different col-

*ors they saw during certain parts of the ceremony and Katherine said she felt more relaxed than usual as she burned her slips of paper. Patrick stated he was surprised when his inner voice told him his second negative thought pattern to be purged; he expected an entirely different theme. I told him that often what we need to release stays hidden from our logical mind until we give ourselves the opportunity to let our psychic self speak. I thanked them all for coming and then took care of the ashes before going to bed.*

You may want to record your Spoken-Word Rituals in your journal. If you choose to do so, particularly focus on noting the purpose for the ceremonies, what written statements you burned (if done), and any images, feelings, or information received during the silent meditation portions. These details can be checked at a future date to verify that your spiritual growth and other personal goals are being accomplished.

## Written-Word Rituals

This next exercise teaches us the importance of using the power of the written word to direct intention, thereby producing desired results. When we release our wishes to the Universal Energies, we tell the cosmic realm we are ready to achieve both short and long-term goals and that we understand the assisting nature of the Universe encompasses spiritual path progression. The Written-Word Ritual helps us not only focus on a goal, but also makes this objective real and attainable.

When performing this writing exercise, it is important to work on one specific issue at a time. To decide which of your goals to use, first do a short meditation to ask yourself what your highest priority is at present. You can also call upon your inner voice and run through your options via the Shower Yes/No exercise (refer to Chapter 3).

We can write a Written-Word Ritual for any and all subjects: career changes, love relationship enhancement, furthering of our life paths, etc. For instance, one can concentrate on this type of intention: "I intend to secure a new job, one which recognizes my creativity and allows me enough freedom to constantly grow and improve my talents."

The exercise consists of five separate steps, listed below. Each paragraph has a distinct theme. The wording listed under each paragraph is only suggested language; feel free to modify it according to your inner voice. When you write out your ritual, start most of your sentences in an affirmative style, beginning with the "I" pronoun (except in subparagraph 2.a.). Be sure to state your intention request very clearly in subparagraph 2.b.

### Creating a Written-Word Ritual

[Note: this exercise is patterned after Science of Mind theory.]

1. Recognition: I recognize the One Source, the Universal Mind.

2. Identification: I identify with this One Source, this Creative Force that permeates my mind, and my mind is One with the One Universal Mind.

> a. This ritual is for (person's name, address, age, physical description, nationality, etc.).

> b. I see this situation as I want it to be. *Describe your intention in detail.*

3. Acceptance: I accept this situation as whole, perfect, complete and in accordance with Divine Plan (Karma) for my soul's spiritual growth in this situation.

4. Thanksgiving: I am indeed thankful to be part of this Cosmos and know that the Universal Laws are operating now. I am thankful to have this knowledge and the right to use it for my own enhancement.

5. Release: I release this request to the Universal Intelligence, the Creative Cosmos, for the completion of the request I have expressed. My responsibility is ended, the situation is perfect, and I have tapped into the One Love that guides us all.

After you are done, it can be very powerful to make a copy of your Written-Word Ritual and then burn it. By burning this duplicate record and scattering the ashes outdoors, you are being assured of truly releasing your intent.

Try working with another goal in a couple of weeks or after your first targeted objective comes to fruition. In our energetic world, intention is the prelude to achieving what we desire, and when you help the process along by doing this hands-on exercise, you are allowing your psychic and higher selves to participate in a very expressive and focused manner.

Whichever type of ritual you choose to perform, as long as you have a clear intention in mind, you will ultimately feel its effectiveness, and will also psychically benefit from reaching out to the Universal Energies. After all, we do exist within a larger Universe that can assist us on our intuitive journey.

# 13

## *Never Underestimate Your Psychic Potential*

Congratulations! You have done a good job in diligently completing some, if not all, of the exercises in this book. The wonderful gift of giving yourself the freedom to uncover and expand your psychic self will have ongoing, far-reaching benefits. At this point, you no doubt feel less burdened by unpleasant past experiences, more intuitively empowered, and more secure with the integration of your spiritual side into your day-to-day world. These were some of my goals for you.

But do not stop here! Continue to regularly practice your meditations and perform again those techniques you enjoyed most. As stated in the Introduction, every one of the exercises presented in this book is designed to deepen your psychic abilities.

There are many other metaphysical modalities and divination methods you may wish to study. After all, by now your appetite is probably whetted to learn even more. Metaphysical tools can greatly enhance and confirm psychic information we receive about ourselves and others. They are called tools because, ideally, they should be used as an adjunct to intuitive messages already obtained—they are not intended to be psychic crutches or stand-alone methodologies.

Exploring some of the tools listed below can be quite helpful to your ongoing psychic education. Most have been used for centuries in this country and around the world. Learning how to work with, and interpret, such modalities will give you a more well-rounded approach to your intuitive side and give you a variety of ways to confirm messages received.

### Additional Metaphysical Tools and Divination Methods

- Rune Stones: A divination method from the Vikings comprised of twenty-five small, rectangular pieces of stone with glyphs carved into them. One first learns the meanings of the glyphs, and then their relationship to one another when laid out in various patterns that address specific issues and questions.

- I-Ching: From the Chinese, meaning "The Book of Change." Yarrow sticks or three coins of the same denomination are thrown and arranged into hexagrams—sixty-four possibilities in all—that are then interpreted according to a highly philosophical and anecdotal reference text.

- Palmistry: Studying the lines, mounds, shapes, and colors of the palms and fingers reveal an immense amount of information about a person. Even the temperature of the skin and backs of the hands are often included in the divination process.

- Astrology: An extremely scientific methodology, astrologers consult myriad charts and tables in a reference book called an *ephemeris*. By doing so, they can obtain detailed information about all areas of one's life, along with specific time periods for the start and completion of life milestones.

- Graphology: Besides being used in psychic readings to gain insight into one's personality, talents, and weaknesses, handwriting analysis is also called upon for more mainstream purposes, like detecting forgery during a court trial or to determine the right candidate for an employment position.

- Hands-on Healing: Directing one's energy into another person can produce beneficial, lasting effects for that client. Both emotional and physical ailments are addressed with this focused, tactile technique. Crystals and tonal sounds (like chanting or striking tuning forks) often are an accompaniment to the process.

- Tarot Cards: Originating in Egypt, the Tarot is a highly visual, symbolic tool full of meaningful, recognizable archetypes and references to numerology. When laid out in patterns, helpful information can be obtained to assist with decision-making and transitioning to one's next life chapter.

- Animal Communication: Besides working with your animal spirit guides, you can learn to meaningfully communicate with living, companion animals too. Having a telepathic conversation with them in their own, pictorial language can uncover any unexpressed wishes or traumatic past experiences they want to share with you.

- Intuitive Medical Diagnosis: Some people possess an innate ability to hone in on physical illnesses present in others, whether or not those being diagnosed are yet cognizant of their diseases. But one also can be trained to intuit medical information, which can then be relayed to the patient's medical practitioner to help develop a protocol for healing.

- Mediumship/Channeling: It can be extremely comforting to receive specific messages from still-loved, departed people and animals who are now in the spirit realm. Learning to have access to these entities provides a much-needed service that helps people gain closure and complete the grieving process.

## The Best is Yet to Come

There is a card in the Tarot deck, entitled The World, that tells us the world is full of magical, wonderful, and unending opportunities just waiting for us to tap into at appropriate and special times in our lives. By viewing your ever-evolving psychic development as The World, you will be assured of a very satisfying and joyful approach to unlocking even more of your intuitive potential. I wish you well on your journey.

# APPENDIX

## *Interpretative Guide to Symbols*

**Where Am I Now?** exercise, Chapter 3.
*Sample responses and their possible meanings follow each symbol.*

## Road = Life Path

A peaceful, beautiful country road can indicate a relaxed attitude toward and enjoyment of your life path. A road overgrown with weeds or strewn with debris can indicate a need to reclaim your life path or clean up any chaotic elements barring you from your life path. A modern, asphalt road can indicate wanting to accelerate the pace to achieving your life path's ultimate purpose, since a concrete road creates a speedy surface.

## Kcy = Knowledge

A skeleton key can indicate ancient wisdom to be uncovered, as well as a possible past-life connection to the time period when this type of key was prevalent. A modern-day key can indicate knowledge to be learned from an upcoming activity, like reading a soul-searching book or attending a self-growth workshop. What you do with the key is also significant: did you keep your need for knowledge close to you? For instance, did you hang the key on a string around your neck or put it in your pocket for easy access?

## Cup = Understanding

An old-style chalice or goblet can indicate information to be obtained from a past life that will help you gain more intuitive understanding. A ceramic mug can indicate the need to be gentler with yourself as you strive to understand your psychic side. After all, mugs are often filled with warm, soothing liquids. A cup made out of a destructible, modern material like plastic or paper can indicate that your current attitude toward understanding your innermost layers is not yet defined or embraced.

## Brook = Sexuality and Creativity

A free-flowing, clear brook can indicate positive feelings about your creative spirit and sexuality. Water that is unmoving or dirty can indicate a necessity to uncover more of your creative abilities and view your sexuality in a more optimistic light. Pebbles or small rocks at the brook's bottom can indicate minor obstacles or setbacks to overcome before enjoying a fulfilling sex life and true creative expression.

## Wall = End of Life, Transition, and Change

The wall's height, length, and shape can indicate how difficult you generally regard transition. Is your wall easy to scale or go around? Is the wall's material pleasing to the eye and touch, or of substandard design and broken in spots? You may have seen a doorway or staircase appear in your wall, which can indicate resourcefulness and readiness to look at your final life chapter. Reflecting upon your wall's description can help you determine if modifications need to be made to your outlook about life changes and death.

# Beyond the Wall = Eternity

Whatever primary components you listed in this paragraph are important to incorporate into your present lifetime. After all, you can begin right now to enjoy the type of setting that will be waiting for you after you cross over into the spirit realm. Do you have a beautiful garden in your eternity scene? Or one filled with animals and joyous people? It is highly significant to acknowledge what kind of environment fills you with peace and encourages you to develop your intuitive side.

# *About the Author*

Rebecca Bloom has eighteen years of experience as a popular teacher of metaphysical subjects. Her company, *Blooming Insights*, helps people develop their intuitive abilities through the application of growth-enhancing techniques and self-study products. Rebecca resides in San Diego, where she enjoys the outdoors with her husband Daniel and their animals.

# Blooming Insights

# Additional Products and Services

To order additional copies of **Begin Your Psychic Journey**, use any of the following options:

- Contact the publisher, www.iUniverse.com.
- Contact www.amazon.com.
- Contact your local bookseller.
- Contact Blooming Insights (see below).

## Also Available
### Expand Your Mind & Soul—Guided Meditations

Includes all of the scripted meditations in *Begin Your Psychic Journey*—plus two more—already narrated for you and set to beautiful, ethereal music. This 60-minute audiocassette is appropriate for both beginners and those already experienced in meditation.
Cost: $12.00 + $1.29 shipping (CA residents also add sales tax).

### Rich in Spirit, Rich in Life: Affirmations for the Five Tenets of Prosperity

Release date: Early 2004

Takes you on a peaceful, instructional journey about the importance of attaining prosperity on many levels. This audio CD also incorporates soothing background music and powerful affirmations to help you achieve the prosperity you deserve. Please contact Blooming Insights to be placed on a confidential, notification e-mail list. [Your e-mail address will never be sold or leased to another party.]

If you are interested in any of the above products or would like to receive information about personal readings, new self-study products, or dates of upcoming workshops, please write or call Blooming Insights:

4113-B Mt. Alifan Dr.
San Diego, CA 92111
(858) 565-1263
bloomingin@cybermesa.com

0-595-29283-6